Table of Contents

Diabetic Diet Cookbook for Beginners UK

150 Budget-Friendly, Nutrient-Rich, and Tasty Diabetic Recipes for Type 2 Diabetes and Prediabetics

Balanced Breakfasts

Mixed Berry Chia Seed Pudding
Yield: 4 servings | Prep time: 10 minutes | Cook time: 0 minutes

Ingredients:

- 240 ml (1 cup) unsweetened almond milk
- 60 ml (1/4 cup) chia seeds
- 5 ml (1 teaspoon) vanilla extract
- 10 ml (2 teaspoons) erythritol or stevia (or another sweetener suitable for diabetics)
- 120 ml (1/2 cup) mixed berries (such as strawberries, raspberries, and blueberries)
- 10 ml (2 teaspoons) desiccated coconut (optional)
- 10 ml (2 teaspoons) chopped nuts (optional)

Directions:

1. In a medium-sized bowl, combine the almond milk, chia seeds, vanilla extract, and sweetener. Mix well.
2. Cover the bowl and refrigerate for at least 4 hours or overnight, until the mixture thickens into a pudding-like consistency.
3. Before serving, stir the pudding to ensure that the chia seeds are evenly distributed.
4. Divide the pudding into four servings. Top each serving with mixed berries, desiccated coconut, and chopped nuts if desired.
5. Serve immediately or store in the refrigerator for up to three days.

Nutritional Information: Approximately 134 calories per serving, 4 g protein, 16 g carbohydrates, 6 g fat, 9 g fiber, 0 mg cholesterol, 56 mg sodium, 119 mg potassium.

Spinach and Feta Egg Muffins
Yield: 6 servings | Prep time: 10 minutes | Cook time: 20 minutes

Ingredients:

- 6 large eggs
- 60 ml (1/4 cup) milk
- 1/4 teaspoon salt
- 1/4 teaspoon black pepper
- 100 g (1 cup) fresh spinach, chopped
- 75 g (3/4 cup) feta cheese, crumbled
- 50 g (1/2 cup) cherry tomatoes, chopped
- 30 g (1/4 cup) red onion, finely diced
- 5 ml (1 teaspoon) olive oil

Directions:

1. Preheat your oven to 180°C (350°F). Grease a 6-cup muffin tin with olive oil.
2. In a medium-sized bowl, whisk together the eggs, milk, salt, and pepper until well combined.
3. Stir in the chopped spinach, crumbled feta cheese, cherry tomatoes, and red onion.
4. Divide the egg mixture evenly among the 6 muffin cups.
5. Bake for 20 minutes, or until the egg muffins are set and a toothpick inserted into the center comes out clean.
6. Allow the muffins to cool in the tin for a few minutes, then use a knife to gently loosen them from the edges of the tin. Serve warm.

Nutritional Information: Approximately 105 calories per serving, 8 g protein, 2 g carbohydrates, 7 g fat, 0.5 g fiber, 189 mg cholesterol, 337 mg sodium, 169 mg potassium.

Greek Yogurt with Roasted Nuts and Berries
Yield: 4 servings | Prep time: 10 minutes | Cook time: 10 minutes

Ingredients:

- 500 g (2 cups) plain Greek yogurt
- 80 g (1/2 cup) mixed berries (strawberries, blueberries, raspberries)
- 40 g (1/4 cup) mixed nuts (almonds, walnuts, pecans)
- 20 g (2 tablespoons) desiccated coconut
- 15 ml (1 tablespoon) honey (optional)
- 2 ml (1/2 teaspoon) cinnamon
- 2 ml (1/2 teaspoon) vanilla extract

Directions:

1. Preheat the oven to 180°C (350°F). Place the mixed nuts on a baking sheet and roast for 10 minutes, or until they are fragrant and golden brown. Remove from the oven and allow them to cool before chopping them into smaller pieces.
2. In a large bowl, mix together the Greek yogurt, cinnamon, and vanilla extract until well combined.
3. Divide the Greek yogurt mixture among four serving bowls.
4. Top each bowl with equal portions of the mixed berries, roasted nuts, desiccated coconut, and a drizzle of honey, if desired.
5. Serve immediately or store in the refrigerator for up to 3 days.

Nutritional Information: Approximately 200 calories per serving, 15 g protein, 12 g carbohydrates, 11 g fat, 2 g fiber, 7 mg cholesterol, 45 mg sodium, 230 mg potassium.

Avocado and Salmon Toast on Whole Grain Bread
Yield: 4 servings | Prep time: 10 minutes | Cook time: 5 minutes

Ingredients:

- 4 slices of whole grain bread
- 2 ripe avocados
- 200 g (7 oz) smoked salmon
- 15 ml (1 tablespoon) lemon juice
- 5 g (1 teaspoon) dill, chopped
- 1/4 teaspoon salt
- 1/4 teaspoon black pepper
- 4 radishes, thinly sliced
- 20 g (1/4 cup) red onion, thinly sliced
- 10 ml (2 teaspoons) capers (optional)

Directions:

1. Toast the whole grain bread until it is crispy and golden brown.
2. In a medium-sized bowl, mash the avocados with the lemon juice, salt, and black pepper until it reaches your desired consistency.
3. Spread the mashed avocado onto each slice of toasted bread.
4. Top each toast with equal portions of smoked salmon, radish slices, red onion slices, and a sprinkle of chopped dill. Add capers if desired.
5. Serve immediately.

Nutritional Information: Approximately 324 calories per serving, 18 g protein, 25 g carbohydrates, 18 g fat, 8 g fiber, 14 mg cholesterol, 869 mg sodium, 681 mg potassium.

Almond and Oat Smoothie Bowl

Yield: 2 servings | Prep time: 5 minutes | Cook time: 0 minutes

Ingredients:

- 240 ml (1 cup) unsweetened almond milk
- 60 g (1/2 cup) rolled oats
- 30 g (1/4 cup) almonds
- 1 ripe banana
- 5 ml (1 teaspoon) vanilla extract
- 5 ml (1 teaspoon) chia seeds
- 10 ml (2 teaspoons) almond butter
- 5 ml (1 teaspoon) honey or a suitable sweetener for diabetics
- 30 g (1/4 cup) mixed berries (blueberries, strawberries, raspberries) for topping
- 10 g (1 tablespoon) coconut flakes for topping (optional)

Directions:

1. In a blender, combine the almond milk, rolled oats, almonds, banana, vanilla extract, chia seeds, almond butter, and sweetener. Blend until smooth and creamy.
2. Pour the smoothie mixture into two bowls.
3. Top each bowl with mixed berries and coconut flakes if desired.
4. Serve immediately.

Nutritional Information: Approximately 326 calories per serving, 9 g protein, 43 g carbohydrates, 14 g fat, 9 g fiber, 0 mg cholesterol, 98 mg sodium, 431 mg potassium.

Quinoa Breakfast Bowl with Fresh Fruit

Yield: 2 servings | Prep time: 10 minutes | Cook time: 15 minutes

Ingredients:

- 90 g (1/2 cup) quinoa, rinsed and drained
- 240 ml (1 cup) water
- 60 ml (1/4 cup) low-fat milk or almond milk
- 30 ml (2 tablespoons) honey or suitable sweetener for diabetics
- 1/2 teaspoon cinnamon
- 1 small apple, diced
- 1 small banana, sliced
- 30 g (1/4 cup) mixed berries (blueberries, strawberries, raspberries)
- 15 g (1 tablespoon) chia seeds
- 15 g (1 tablespoon) flax seeds
- 15 g (1 tablespoon) pumpkin seeds

Directions:

1. In a small saucepan, bring the water to a boil. Add the quinoa, reduce the heat to low, cover, and simmer for about 15 minutes, or until the quinoa is cooked and the water has been absorbed.
2. Remove the saucepan from the heat and let it sit for a few minutes, then fluff the quinoa with a fork.
3. In a small bowl, whisk together the milk, honey or sweetener, and cinnamon.
4. Divide the cooked quinoa between two bowls. Pour the milk mixture over the quinoa in each bowl.
5. Top each bowl with the diced apple, banana slices, mixed berries, chia seeds, flax seeds, and pumpkin seeds.
6. Serve immediately.

Nutritional Information: Approximately 386 calories per serving, 11 g protein, 73 g carbohydrates, 8 g fat, 9 g fiber, 1 mg cholesterol, 12 mg sodium, 676 mg potassium.

Low-carb Cauliflower Hash Browns

Yield: 4 servings | Prep time: 15 minutes | Cook time: 20 minutes

Ingredients:

- 1 medium cauliflower, grated or finely chopped (about 400 g)
- 1 large egg
- 30 g (1/4 cup) grated Parmesan cheese
- 30 g (1/4 cup) almond flour
- 5 g (1 teaspoon) garlic powder
- 5 g (1 teaspoon) onion powder
- 1/4 teaspoon salt
- 1/4 teaspoon black pepper
- 30 ml (2 tablespoons) olive oil

Directions:

1. Preheat the oven to 200°C (400°F) and line a baking sheet with parchment paper.
2. Place the grated cauliflower in a microwave-safe bowl and microwave on high for 4 minutes, or until tender. Allow it to cool for a few minutes.
3. Place the cauliflower in a clean tea towel and squeeze out as much moisture as possible.
4. In a large bowl, combine the cauliflower, egg, Parmesan cheese, almond flour, garlic powder, onion powder, salt, and black pepper. Mix well.
5. Form the mixture into 8 equal-sized patties and place them on the prepared baking sheet.
6. Brush each patty with olive oil and bake for about 20 minutes, or until they are golden brown and crispy.
7. Serve immediately.

Nutritional Information: Approximately 130 calories per serving, 7 g protein, 9 g carbohydrates, 9 g fat, 3 g fiber, 45 mg cholesterol, 330 mg sodium, 354 mg potassium.

Sugar-free Granola with Greek Yogurt

Yield: 4 servings | Prep time: 10 minutes | Cook time: 20 minutes

Ingredients:

- 200 g (2 cups) rolled oats
- 60 g (1/2 cup) nuts (almonds, walnuts, pecans), roughly chopped
- 30 g (1/4 cup) seeds (sunflower seeds, pumpkin seeds, chia seeds)
- 1 teaspoon ground cinnamon
- 1/4 teaspoon salt
- 60 ml (1/4 cup) coconut oil, melted
- 60 ml (1/4 cup) sugar-free maple syrup
- 1 teaspoon vanilla extract
- 200 g (1 cup) plain Greek yogurt
- 100 g (1 cup) mixed berries (blueberries, strawberries, raspberries)

Directions:

1. Preheat your oven to 180°C (350°F) and line a baking sheet with parchment paper.
2. In a large bowl, mix together the rolled oats, chopped nuts, seeds, cinnamon, and salt.
3. In a small bowl, whisk together the melted coconut oil, sugar-free maple syrup, and vanilla extract.
4. Pour the wet ingredients into the dry ingredients and stir well to combine.
5. Spread the granola mixture evenly on the prepared baking sheet.
6. Bake for about 20 minutes, stirring halfway through, until the granola is golden brown.
7. Allow the granola to cool completely on the baking sheet.
8. To serve, spoon the Greek yogurt into bowls and top with the granola and mixed berries.

Nutritional Information: Approximately 403 calories per serving, 14 g protein, 39 g carbohydrates, 22 g fat, 6 g fiber, 5 mg cholesterol, 166 mg sodium, 355 mg potassium.

Smoked Mackerel and Scrambled Eggs

Yield: 2 servings | Prep time: 5 minutes | Cook time: 5 minutes

Ingredients:

- 2 smoked mackerel fillets (approximately 200 g)
- 4 large eggs
- 30 ml (2 tablespoons) milk
- Salt and pepper, to taste
- 15 g (1 tablespoon) unsalted butter
- 10 g (2 tablespoons) chopped fresh chives
- 2 slices of whole-grain toast (optional)

Directions:

1. Flake the smoked mackerel fillets into small pieces and set aside.
2. In a medium bowl, beat the eggs with the milk and season with salt and pepper.
3. In a nonstick skillet, melt the butter over medium-low heat.
4. Add the beaten eggs to the skillet and cook, stirring constantly, until soft curds form, about 2-3 minutes.
5. Just before the eggs are fully cooked, stir in the flaked mackerel and chives, and cook for an additional 1-2 minutes, until the mackerel is heated through.
6. Serve the scrambled eggs and mackerel on whole-grain toast, if desired.

Nutritional Information: Approximately 315 calories per serving, 33 g protein, 2 g carbohydrates, 20 g fat, 0 g fiber, 285 mg cholesterol, 900 mg sodium, 420 mg potassium.

Zucchini and Cheese Frittata

Yield: 4 servings | Prep time: 10 minutes | Cook time: 15 minutes

Ingredients:

- 4 medium zucchinis (approximately 400 g), sliced thinly
- 6 large eggs
- 60 ml (1/4 cup) skimmed milk
- 100 g (1 cup) grated low-fat cheese (cheddar or mozzarella)
- 2 tablespoons fresh basil, chopped
- Salt and pepper, to taste
- 15 g (1 tablespoon) olive oil
- 10 g (2 tablespoons) grated Parmesan cheese (optional)

Directions:

1. Preheat the oven to 180°C (350°F).
2. In a large bowl, beat the eggs with the milk, grated cheese, basil, salt, and pepper.
3. Heat the olive oil in an oven-safe skillet over medium heat. Add the zucchini slices and cook, stirring occasionally, until softened, about 5 minutes.
4. Pour the egg mixture over the zucchini and cook for 2-3 minutes until the edges are set.
5. Sprinkle the top with grated Parmesan cheese, if desired.
6. Transfer the skillet to the preheated oven and bake for about 10 minutes, or until the frittata is set and lightly golden.
7. Let the frittata cool for a few minutes, then slice and serve.

Nutritional Information: Approximately 212 calories per serving, 17 g protein, 9 g carbohydrates, 12 g fat, 2 g fiber, 300 mg cholesterol, 350 mg sodium, 430 mg potassium.

Steel-Cut Oats with Cinnamon and Apples
Yield: 4 servings | Prep time: 10 minutes | Cook time: 30 minutes

Ingredients:

- 200 g (1 cup) steel-cut oats
- 1 litre (4 cups) water
- 2 medium apples (approximately 200 g), cored and diced
- 5 g (1 teaspoon) ground cinnamon
- 5 ml (1 teaspoon) vanilla extract
- Pinch of salt
- 80 ml (1/3 cup) skimmed milk
- Optional toppings: chopped nuts, seeds, Greek yogurt

Directions:

1. In a large saucepan, bring the water and salt to a boil. Slowly add the steel-cut oats, stirring constantly to prevent clumps from forming.
2. Reduce the heat to low and simmer the oats for about 25-30 minutes, stirring occasionally, until they're cooked and have a creamy texture.
3. While the oats are cooking, place the diced apples in a microwave-safe bowl, sprinkle with cinnamon, and microwave for 2-3 minutes until softened.
4. Once the oats are cooked, remove the saucepan from the heat and stir in the vanilla extract and skimmed milk.
5. Serve the oats in bowls, topped with the cinnamon apples and any additional toppings of your choice.

Nutritional Information: Approximately 220 calories per serving, 8 g protein, 45 g carbohydrates, 3 g fat, 6 g fiber, 1 mg cholesterol, 20 mg sodium, 150 mg potassium.

Smoked Salmon and Cream Cheese Bagel
Yield: 2 servings | Prep time: 5 minutes | Cook time: 5 minutes

Ingredients:

- 2 whole-grain bagels (approximately 160 g)
- 100 g smoked salmon
- 60 g light cream cheese
- 1/2 small red onion (approximately 50 g), thinly sliced
- 1 medium-sized tomato (approximately 100 g), thinly sliced
- 10 g fresh dill, finely chopped
- 1/2 lemon, zest and juice
- Freshly ground black pepper, to taste

Directions:

1. Preheat the oven to 180°C (350°F) and toast the whole-grain bagels for about 5 minutes, or until they're crispy and golden-brown.
2. While the bagels are toasting, in a small bowl, combine the light cream cheese, lemon zest, lemon juice, and freshly ground black pepper. Mix until smooth and creamy.
3. Once the bagels are toasted, spread the cream cheese mixture evenly on each half.
4. Layer the smoked salmon, thinly sliced red onion, and sliced tomatoes on top of the cream cheese.
5. Garnish with the chopped dill and serve immediately.

Nutritional Information: Approximately 325 calories per serving, 20 g protein, 45 g carbohydrates, 9 g fat, 7 g fiber, 25 mg cholesterol, 800 mg sodium, 320 mg potassium

Protein-Packed Pancakes with Almond Butter

Yield: 4 servings | Prep time: 10 minutes | Cook time: 15 minutes

Ingredients:

- 200 g Greek yogurt
- 100 g rolled oats
- 100 g whole wheat flour
- 2 large eggs
- 60 ml almond milk
- 2 tbsp protein powder (unsweetened)
- 1 tsp baking powder
- 1/2 tsp vanilla extract
- 1/4 tsp salt
- Olive oil spray, for cooking
- 80 g almond butter
- Fresh berries, for serving (optional)

Directions:

1. In a blender, combine the Greek yogurt, rolled oats, whole wheat flour, eggs, almond milk, protein powder, baking powder, vanilla extract, and salt. Blend until smooth.
2. Preheat a non-stick pan over medium heat and lightly spray with olive oil.
3. Pour a ladleful of batter onto the pan and cook for 2-3 minutes until small bubbles form on the surface. Flip and cook for another 2-3 minutes until golden brown. Repeat with the remaining batter.
4. Serve the pancakes warm, topped with almond butter and fresh berries, if desired.

Nutritional Information: Approximately 350 calories per serving, 20 g protein, 35 g carbohydrates, 18 g fat, 6 g fiber, 90 mg cholesterol, 250 mg sodium, 270 mg potassium.

Turkey Bacon and Veggie Breakfast Burrito

Yield: 4 servings | Prep time: 15 minutes | Cook time: 15 minutes

Ingredients:

- 8 slices of turkey bacon
- 1 tbsp olive oil
- 1 small red onion, chopped (about 70 g)
- 1 red bell pepper, chopped (about 150 g)
- 1 green bell pepper, chopped (about 150 g)
- 4 large eggs, beaten
- 1/2 tsp black pepper
- 4 whole grain tortillas (about 200 g total)
- 100 g reduced-fat cheddar cheese, shredded
- 60 g salsa (optional)
- 2 tbsp fresh coriander, chopped (optional)

Directions:

1. In a large non-stick skillet, cook the turkey bacon over medium heat until crispy, about 5 minutes. Remove from the skillet and set aside.
2. In the same skillet, add the olive oil and heat over medium heat. Add the onion and bell peppers and cook until softened, about 5 minutes.
3. Pour the beaten eggs into the skillet with the vegetables. Season with black pepper and scramble until cooked through, about 3-4 minutes.
4. Warm the tortillas in the microwave or on a dry skillet over low heat for about 30 seconds.
5. Divide the scrambled eggs and vegetables among the tortillas. Sprinkle with cheddar cheese and crumble the turkey bacon on top. Add salsa and fresh coriander if desired.
6. Fold in the sides of the tortilla and roll up to form a burrito. Serve immediately.

Nutritional Information: Approximately 340 calories per serving, 21 g protein, 30 g carbohydrates, 16 g fat, 4 g fiber, 220 mg cholesterol, 740 mg sodium, 350 mg potassium.

Spinach and Mushroom Omelette
Yield: 2 servings | Prep time: 10 minutes | Cook time: 10 minutes

Ingredients:

- 4 large eggs
- 2 tbsp water
- 1/4 tsp black pepper
- 1/4 tsp salt (optional)
- 1 tbsp olive oil

- 200 g fresh mushrooms, sliced
- 150 g fresh spinach, roughly chopped
- 50 g reduced-fat cheddar cheese, shredded
- 2 tbsp fresh parsley, chopped (optional)

Directions:

1. In a bowl, whisk together the eggs, water, black pepper, and salt (if using). Set aside.
2. In a non-stick skillet, heat the olive oil over medium heat. Add the mushrooms and sauté until they release their liquid and start to brown, about 5 minutes.
3. Add the spinach to the skillet and cook until wilted, about 2 minutes.
4. Pour the egg mixture into the skillet, covering the vegetables evenly. Cook without stirring until the edges are set, about 2-3 minutes.
5. Sprinkle the cheese over one half of the omelette. Using a spatula, carefully fold the other half of the omelette over the cheese.
6. Cook for an additional 2-3 minutes, until the omelette is fully set and the cheese is melted. Serve garnished with fresh parsley if desired.

Nutritional Information: Approximately 280 calories per serving, 22 g protein, 6 g carbohydrates, 20 g fat, 2 g fiber, 400 mg cholesterol, 450 mg sodium, 650 mg potassium.

Breakfast Quesadilla with Avocado
Yield: 2 servings | Prep time: 10 minutes | Cook time: 10 minutes

Ingredients:

- 2 whole grain tortillas (approx. 20 cm in diameter)
- 4 large eggs
- 1/4 tsp black pepper
- 1/4 tsp salt (optional)
- 1 tbsp olive oil

- 100 g reduced-fat cheddar cheese, shredded
- 1 medium avocado, pitted, peeled, and sliced
- 100 g cherry tomatoes, halved
- 50 g fresh coriander, chopped
- 1 lime, cut into wedges

Directions:

1. In a bowl, whisk together the eggs, black pepper, and salt (if using). Set aside.
2. In a non-stick skillet, heat the olive oil over medium heat. Add the egg mixture and scramble until cooked through. Remove from the skillet and set aside.
3. Place one tortilla in the skillet. Sprinkle half of the cheese over one half of the tortilla. Top with half of the scrambled eggs, half of the avocado slices, half of the cherry tomatoes, and half of the coriander. Fold the other half of the tortilla over the filling.
4. Cook for 2-3 minutes on each side, until the tortilla is golden brown and the cheese is melted. Repeat with the remaining tortilla and filling.
5. Cut each quesadilla into wedges and serve with lime wedges on the side.

Nutritional Information: Approximately 450 calories per serving, 22 g protein, 40 g carbohydrates, 24 g fat, 10 g fiber, 400 mg cholesterol, 550 mg sodium, 700 mg potassium.

Savoury Breakfast Muffins
Yield: 6 servings | Prep time: 15 minutes | Cook time: 25 minutes

Ingredients:

- 150 g whole wheat flour
- 50 g rolled oats
- 2 tsp baking powder
- 1/4 tsp salt
- 1/4 tsp black pepper
- 2 large eggs
- 150 ml low-fat milk
- 60 ml olive oil
- 50 g reduced-fat cheddar cheese, grated
- 100 g spinach, chopped
- 50 g red bell pepper, finely diced
- 50 g mushrooms, finely diced
- 2 spring onions, chopped

Directions:

1. Preheat the oven to 180°C. Grease or line a 6-cup muffin tin with paper liners.
2. In a large bowl, combine the whole wheat flour, rolled oats, baking powder, salt, and black pepper.
3. In a separate bowl, whisk together the eggs, milk, and olive oil. Add the wet ingredients to the dry ingredients and stir until just combined.
4. Fold in the grated cheese, spinach, red bell pepper, mushrooms, and spring onions.
5. Divide the batter evenly among the prepared muffin cups.
6. Bake for 25 minutes, or until a toothpick inserted into the center of a muffin comes out clean.
7. Allow the muffins to cool in the tin for 5 minutes before transferring them to a wire rack to cool completely.

Nutritional Information: Approximately 210 calories per serving, 8 g protein, 23 g carbohydrates, 10 g fat, 4 g fiber, 75 mg cholesterol, 300 mg sodium, 250 mg potassium.

Strawberry and Almond Breakfast Parfait
Yield: 4 servings | Prep time: 10 minutes | Cook time: 0 minutes

Ingredients:

- 200 g fresh strawberries, hulled and sliced
- 400 g Greek yogurt, low-fat
- 50 g almonds, roasted and chopped
- 20 g chia seeds
- 2 tsp vanilla extract
- 2 tbsp almond butter
- 4 mint leaves, for garnish

Directions:

1. In a medium-sized bowl, combine the Greek yogurt, chia seeds, and vanilla extract. Stir until well combined and set aside for 5 minutes to let the chia seeds expand.
2. Take four serving glasses or jars. Layer the bottom of each glass with a spoonful of the Greek yogurt mixture.
3. Add a layer of sliced strawberries on top of the yogurt layer.
4. Add another layer of the Greek yogurt mixture on top of the strawberries.
5. Sprinkle some chopped almonds on top.
6. Repeat the layers until the glasses are full, finishing with a layer of strawberries and almonds on top.
7. Drizzle each parfait with almond butter and garnish with a mint leaf.
8. Serve immediately or refrigerate for up to 2 hours before serving.

Nutritional Information: Approximately 230 calories per serving, 13 g protein, 18 g carbohydrates, 13 g fat, 5 g fiber, 10 mg cholesterol, 40 mg sodium, 350 mg potassium.

Warm Breakfast Salad with Spinach and Poached Eggs

Yield: 4 servings | Prep time: 10 minutes | Cook time: 10 minutes

Ingredients:

- 4 large eggs
- 200 g baby spinach leaves
- 200 g cherry tomatoes, halved
- 100 g mushrooms, sliced
- 1 small red onion, thinly sliced
- 2 tbsp olive oil
- 2 tbsp white wine vinegar
- 1 tsp Dijon mustard
- Salt and pepper, to taste
- 4 slices whole-grain bread, toasted
- 2 tbsp freshly grated Parmesan cheese (optional)

Directions:

1. Fill a medium-sized saucepan with water and bring it to a simmer. Add the white wine vinegar and a pinch of salt. Crack the eggs one by one into separate small bowls, then gently slide them into the simmering water. Poach for 3-4 minutes or until the whites are set and the yolks remain runny. Remove with a slotted spoon and drain on paper towels.
2. While the eggs are poaching, heat 1 tablespoon of olive oil in a large skillet over medium heat. Add the sliced mushrooms and cook until they release their liquid and turn golden brown, about 4-5 minutes. Add the cherry tomatoes and cook for another 2 minutes. Season with salt and pepper.
3. In a large bowl, combine the baby spinach and red onion. Add the cooked mushrooms and tomatoes.
4. In a small bowl, whisk together the remaining 1 tablespoon of olive oil, Dijon mustard, salt, and pepper. Drizzle the dressing over the salad and toss to combine.
5. Divide the salad among four plates, and top each with a poached egg. Serve with a slice of toasted whole-grain bread and a sprinkle of freshly grated Parmesan cheese, if desired.

Nutritional Information: Approximately 280 calories per serving, 14 g protein, 22 g carbohydrates, 16 g fat, 4 g fiber, 190 mg cholesterol, 390 mg sodium, 450 mg potassium.

Satisfying Soups and Stews

Creamy Cauliflower and Leek Soup

Yield: 4 servings | Prep time: 15 minutes | Cook time: 30 minutes

Ingredients:

- 1 large cauliflower (about 800 g), chopped into florets
- 2 large leeks, cleaned and chopped
- 1 medium onion, chopped
- 2 cloves garlic, minced
- 1 litre low-sodium vegetable broth
- 240 ml unsweetened almond milk
- 2 tbsp olive oil
- Salt and pepper, to taste
- 1 tsp dried thyme
- 1 tsp dried rosemary
- Chopped fresh parsley for garnish

Directions:

1. In a large pot, heat the olive oil over medium heat. Add the leeks, onion, and garlic and sauté until softened, about 5 minutes.
2. Add the cauliflower florets to the pot along with the vegetable broth, dried thyme, and dried rosemary. Bring to a simmer, cover, and cook until the cauliflower is tender, about 15-20 minutes.
3. Use an immersion blender to purée the soup until smooth, or transfer the soup to a blender in batches and blend until smooth. Return the soup to the pot if using a blender.
4. Stir in the almond milk and season with salt and pepper. Heat the soup gently over low heat until warmed through.
5. Serve the soup hot, garnished with chopped fresh parsley.

Nutritional Information: Approximately 135 calories per serving, 4 g protein, 22 g carbohydrates, 5 g fat, 5 g fiber, 0 mg cholesterol, 410 mg sodium, 800 mg potassium.

Tuscan White Bean and Kale Soup

Yield: 6 servings | Prep time: 15 minutes | Cook time: 30 minutes

Ingredients:

- 400 g canned cannellini beans, drained and rinsed
- 1 large onion, diced
- 2 cloves garlic, minced
- 1 large carrot, diced
- 2 celery stalks, diced
- 150 g kale, stems removed and leaves chopped
- 1.5 litres low-sodium vegetable broth
- 400 g canned diced tomatoes
- 2 tbsp olive oil
- 1 tsp dried thyme
- 1 tsp dried rosemary
- Salt and pepper, to taste
- Grated Parmesan cheese, for garnish (optional)

Directions:

1. In a large pot, heat the olive oil over medium heat. Add the onion, carrot, and celery and sauté for about 5 minutes, until the vegetables start to soften. Add the garlic and continue to sauté for another 2 minutes.
2. Add the beans, kale, vegetable broth, diced tomatoes, thyme, and rosemary to the pot. Bring the soup to a simmer, then reduce the heat to low, cover, and let it simmer for 20 minutes, stirring occasionally.
3. Season the soup with salt and pepper to taste. If desired, use an immersion blender to partially blend the soup, leaving some beans and vegetables whole for texture.
4. Serve the soup hot, garnished with grated Parmesan cheese if desired.

Nutritional Information: Approximately 200 calories per serving, 9 g protein, 28 g carbohydrates, 7 g fat, 7 g fiber, 0 mg cholesterol, 420 mg sodium, 600 mg potassium.

Hearty Lentil and Vegetable Stew

Yield: 6 servings | Prep time: 15 minutes | Cook time: 40 minutes

Ingredients:

- 200 g dried green or brown lentils, rinsed and drained
- 1 large onion, diced
- 2 large carrots, peeled and diced
- 2 celery stalks, diced
- 2 cloves garlic, minced
- 1 medium zucchini, diced
- 1 red bell pepper, diced
- 1 yellow bell pepper, diced
- 400 g canned diced tomatoes
- 1.5 litres low-sodium vegetable broth
- 2 tbsp olive oil
- 1 tsp dried basil
- 1 tsp dried thyme
- Salt and pepper, to taste
- Chopped fresh parsley, for garnish

Directions:

1. In a large pot, heat the olive oil over medium heat. Add the onion, carrots, and celery and sauté for about 5 minutes, until the vegetables start to soften. Add the garlic and continue to sauté for another 2 minutes.
2. Add the lentils, zucchini, bell peppers, canned tomatoes, vegetable broth, basil, and thyme to the pot. Bring the stew to a simmer, then reduce the heat to low, cover, and let it simmer for 30 minutes, stirring occasionally.
3. Check the lentils for doneness; they should be tender but not mushy. Season the stew with salt and pepper to taste.
4. Serve the stew hot, garnished with chopped fresh parsley.

Nutritional Information: Approximately 220 calories per serving, 12 g protein, 38 g carbohydrates, 4 g fat, 10 g fiber, 0 mg cholesterol, 360 mg sodium, 720 mg potassium.

Rich Beef and Vegetable Soup

Yield: 6 servings | Prep time: 15 minutes | Cook time: 2 hours

Ingredients:

- 500 g lean stewing beef, cubed
- 1 large onion, chopped
- 3 cloves garlic, minced
- 2 carrots, chopped
- 2 celery stalks, chopped
- 200 g green beans, chopped
- 1 red bell pepper, chopped
- 400 g canned chopped tomatoes
- 1.5 litres beef broth, low sodium
- 2 tbsp olive oil
- 1 tsp dried oregano
- 1 tsp dried basil
- Salt and pepper, to taste
- Fresh parsley, chopped, for garnish

Directions:

1. In a large pot, heat the olive oil over medium-high heat. Add the beef and brown on all sides. Remove the beef and set it aside.
2. In the same pot, add the onion, garlic, carrots, and celery. Sauté for about 5 minutes until the vegetables start to soften.
3. Return the beef to the pot. Add the green beans, bell pepper, chopped tomatoes, beef broth, oregano, and basil. Season with salt and pepper to taste.
4. Bring the soup to a boil, then reduce the heat to low, cover, and let it simmer for about 1.5 hours, stirring occasionally.
5. Serve the soup hot, garnished with chopped parsley.

Nutritional Information: Approximately 220 calories per serving, 20 g protein, 15 g carbohydrates, 8 g fat, 4 g fiber, 50 mg cholesterol, 450 mg sodium, 650 mg potassium.

Classic Chicken Noodle Soup (with Zucchini Noodles)
Yield: 6 servings | Prep time: 15 minutes | Cook time: 30 minutes

Ingredients:

- 500 g skinless, boneless chicken breast
- 2 medium-sized zucchinis, spiralized into noodles
- 1 large onion, chopped
- 3 cloves garlic, minced
- 2 carrots, chopped
- 3 celery stalks, chopped
- 1.5 litres chicken broth, low sodium
- 2 tbsp olive oil
- 1 tsp dried thyme
- 1 tsp dried rosemary
- Salt and pepper, to taste
- Fresh parsley, chopped, for garnish

Directions:

1. In a large pot, heat the olive oil over medium-high heat. Add the chicken breasts and cook until browned on both sides, about 4 minutes per side. Remove the chicken and set it aside.
2. In the same pot, add the onion, garlic, carrots, and celery. Sauté for about 5 minutes until the vegetables start to soften.
3. Return the chicken to the pot. Add the chicken broth, thyme, and rosemary. Season with salt and pepper to taste.
4. Bring the soup to a boil, then reduce the heat to low, cover, and let it simmer for about 20 minutes, stirring occasionally.
5. Remove the chicken from the pot, shred it with two forks, and return it to the soup.
6. Add the zucchini noodles to the soup and cook for an additional 2 minutes until the noodles are just tender.
7. Serve the soup hot, garnished with chopped parsley.

Nutritional Information: Approximately 180 calories per serving, 25 g protein, 12 g carbohydrates, 4 g fat, 2 g fiber, 50 mg cholesterol, 350 mg sodium, 500 mg potassium.

Creamy Pumpkin and Ginger Soup
Yield: 4 servings | Prep time: 15 minutes | Cook time: 30 minutes

Ingredients:

- 800 g pumpkin, peeled, deseeded, and chopped into cubes
- 1 medium-sized onion, chopped
- 2 cloves garlic, minced
- 1 thumb-sized piece of ginger, grated
- 1 litre vegetable or chicken broth, low sodium
- 200 ml coconut milk, light
- 1 tbsp olive oil
- 1/2 tsp ground nutmeg
- Salt and pepper, to taste
- Fresh coriander, for garnish

Directions:

1. In a large pot, heat the olive oil over medium heat. Add the onions and cook until translucent, about 3 minutes. Add the garlic and ginger and cook for another minute, stirring continuously.
2. Add the pumpkin cubes, broth, nutmeg, salt, and pepper to the pot. Bring the soup to a boil, then reduce the heat and simmer for about 20 minutes, until the pumpkin is soft and easily pierced with a fork.
3. Remove the soup from the heat and use an immersion blender to puree the soup until smooth. If you don't have an immersion blender, you can transfer the soup to a countertop blender and blend in batches.
4. Stir in the coconut milk and heat the soup over low heat until it's warmed through. Taste and adjust the seasoning, if necessary. Serve the soup hot, garnished with fresh coriander.

Nutritional Information: Approximately 150 calories per serving, 3 g protein, 25 g carbohydrates, 5 g fat, 4 g fiber, 0 mg cholesterol, 300 mg sodium, 600 mg potassium.

Fragrant Thai Coconut Soup

Yield: 4 servings | Prep time: 15 minutes | Cook time: 25 minutes

Ingredients:

- 400 ml light coconut milk
- 1 litre chicken or vegetable broth, low sodium
- 300 g chicken breast, skinless and boneless, thinly sliced
- 200 g mushrooms, sliced
- 100 g snow peas, sliced
- 1 medium-sized red bell pepper, sliced
- 1 small onion, thinly sliced
- 3 cloves garlic, minced
- 1 thumb-sized piece of ginger, grated
- 1 stalk lemongrass, finely chopped
- 2 tbsp fish sauce
- 1 tbsp lime juice
- 1 tsp red chili flakes
- 2 tsp brown sugar or stevia
- Fresh coriander, for garnish
- Salt, to taste

Directions:

1. In a large pot, bring the chicken or vegetable broth to a boil. Add the lemongrass, ginger, and garlic, and simmer for about 5 minutes.
2. Add the chicken, mushrooms, snow peas, bell pepper, and onion to the pot. Let the soup simmer for another 10 minutes, until the chicken is cooked through and the vegetables are tender.
3. Stir in the coconut milk, fish sauce, lime juice, red chili flakes, and sugar or stevia. Cook for an additional 5 minutes.
4. Season the soup with salt to taste, and serve hot, garnished with fresh coriander.

Nutritional Information: Approximately 200 calories per serving, 20 g protein, 12 g carbohydrates, 9 g fat, 2 g fiber, 40 mg cholesterol, 800 mg sodium, 400 mg potassium.

Rustic Potato and Leek Soup

Yield: 6 servings | Prep time: 15 minutes | Cook time: 35 minutes

Ingredients:

- 500 g potatoes, peeled and diced
- 3 leeks, cleaned and sliced (white and light green parts only)
- 2 cloves garlic, minced
- 1.5 litres vegetable broth, low-sodium
- 2 tablespoons olive oil
- 1 teaspoon dried thyme
- 1 bay leaf
- Salt and pepper to taste
- Fresh parsley, chopped (for garnish)
- 100 ml skimmed milk or unsweetened almond milk

Directions:

1. In a large pot, heat the olive oil over medium heat. Add the sliced leeks and sauté until soft and translucent, about 5-7 minutes. Add the minced garlic and sauté for another 1-2 minutes.
2. Add the diced potatoes, vegetable broth, thyme, and bay leaf to the pot. Season with salt and pepper to taste. Bring the soup to a boil, then reduce the heat and simmer for 25-30 minutes, or until the potatoes are tender.
3. Remove the bay leaf and discard it. Use an immersion blender or a regular blender to partially blend the soup, leaving some chunks of potato and leek for a rustic texture.
4. Stir in the milk and heat the soup over low heat until warmed through. Adjust the seasoning if needed.
5. Serve the soup in bowls, garnished with fresh parsley.

Nutritional Information: Approximately 150 calories per serving, 3 g protein, 27 g carbohydrates, 3 g fat, 4 g fiber, 0 mg cholesterol, 350 mg sodium, 600 mg potassium.

Spicy Moroccan Chickpea Stew
Yield: 4 servings | Prep time: 15 minutes | Cook time: 35 minutes

Ingredients:

- 2 tbsp olive oil
- 1 large onion, chopped
- 3 cloves garlic, minced
- 2 medium carrots, peeled and diced
- 2 medium red bell peppers, diced
- 400 g canned chickpeas, drained and rinsed
- 400 g canned tomatoes, diced
- 750 ml vegetable broth, low sodium
- 2 tsp ground cumin
- 2 tsp ground coriander
- 1 tsp ground turmeric
- 1 tsp ground paprika
- 1/2 tsp ground cinnamon
- 1/2 tsp cayenne pepper
- Salt and pepper, to taste
- 1 handful fresh coriander, chopped
- 1 lemon, juiced

Directions:

1. In a large pot, heat the olive oil over medium heat. Add the onions and garlic and cook for about 3 minutes, until the onions are translucent.
2. Add the carrots and bell peppers and cook for another 5 minutes until the vegetables begin to soften.
3. Stir in the chickpeas, tomatoes, vegetable broth, cumin, coriander, turmeric, paprika, cinnamon, cayenne pepper, salt, and pepper. Bring the stew to a boil.
4. Reduce the heat to low and let the stew simmer for about 25 minutes, stirring occasionally, until the vegetables are tender.
5. Stir in the fresh coriander and lemon juice.
6. Serve hot, on its own or with whole grain bread or a side of quinoa.

Nutritional Information: Approximately 240 calories per serving, 8 g protein, 40 g carbohydrates, 6 g fat, 10 g fiber, 0 mg cholesterol, 400 mg sodium, 650 mg potassium.

Miso Soup with Tofu and Seaweed
Yield: 4 servings | Prep time: 10 minutes | Cook time: 10 minutes

Ingredients:

- 4 cups (1 litre) water
- 1/4 cup (60 ml) miso paste (reduced sodium if available)
- 200 g tofu, cubed
- 1 sheet nori seaweed, cut into small pieces
- 2 spring onions, thinly sliced
- 1 teaspoon sesame oil
- 2 tablespoons dried wakame seaweed
- 1 teaspoon fresh ginger, grated

Directions:

1. In a medium-sized pot, bring the water to a simmer. Do not let it boil.
2. In a small bowl, dissolve the miso paste in a few tablespoons of the hot water to create a smooth paste. Add the miso paste to the pot and stir until dissolved.
3. Add the tofu, nori seaweed, dried wakame, ginger, and sesame oil to the pot. Simmer for about 5 minutes, or until the wakame has rehydrated and the soup is hot.
4. Remove from heat and serve immediately, garnished with the sliced spring onions.

Nutritional Information: Approximately 80 calories per serving, 6 g protein, 7 g carbohydrates, 2.5 g fat, 2 g fiber, 0 mg cholesterol, 600 mg sodium, 150 mg potassium.

Hearty Minestrone Soup
Yield: 4 servings | Prep time: 15 minutes | Cook time: 30 minutes

Ingredients:

- 2 tbsp olive oil
- 1 medium onion, chopped
- 2 cloves garlic, minced
- 2 medium carrots, peeled and diced
- 2 medium celery stalks, diced
- 1 medium zucchini, diced
- 400 g canned tomatoes, diced
- 750 ml vegetable broth, low sodium
- 100 g whole grain pasta, such as penne or fusilli
- 200 g canned cannellini beans, drained and rinsed
- 100 g fresh spinach leaves, chopped
- 2 tsp dried oregano
- 2 tsp dried basil
- Salt and pepper, to taste
- 1 handful fresh basil leaves, chopped
- 1 tbsp grated Parmesan cheese (optional)

Directions:

1. In a large pot, heat the olive oil over medium heat. Add the onions and garlic and sauté until translucent, about 3 minutes.
2. Add the carrots and celery and cook for another 5 minutes.
3. Stir in the zucchini, canned tomatoes, vegetable broth, pasta, cannellini beans, chopped spinach, oregano, dried basil, salt, and pepper. Bring to a boil.
4. Reduce the heat to low and simmer for about 20 minutes, stirring occasionally, until the vegetables and pasta are tender.
5. Stir in the fresh basil and adjust the seasoning if needed.
6. Serve the soup hot, optionally garnished with grated Parmesan cheese.

Nutritional Information: Approximately 220 calories per serving, 8 g protein, 35 g carbohydrates, 6 g fat, 8 g fiber, 5 mg cholesterol (if using Parmesan), 450 mg sodium, 600 mg potassium.

French Onion Soup with Cheese Croutons
Yield: 4 servings | Prep time: 15 minutes | Cook time: 45 minutes

Ingredients:

- 4 medium onions, thinly sliced
- 2 tablespoons olive oil
- 2 cloves garlic, minced
- 1 litre low-sodium beef broth
- 240 ml dry red wine (optional)
- 2 teaspoons fresh thyme leaves, chopped
- 4 slices whole-grain bread
- 100 g grated low-fat cheese (e.g., mozzarella or gruyere)
- Salt and pepper to taste
- Fresh parsley, chopped (for garnish)

Directions:

1. In a large pot, heat the olive oil over medium heat. Add the sliced onions and cook, stirring occasionally, until they are caramelised and golden brown, about 25-30 minutes.
2. Stir in the garlic and cook for an additional minute. Add the beef broth, red wine (if using), and thyme. Bring the soup to a boil.
3. Reduce the heat to low and let it simmer for 15 minutes. Season with salt and pepper to taste.
4. While the soup is simmering, toast the slices of whole-grain bread. Sprinkle the grated cheese on top of each slice and place under a grill until the cheese is melted and bubbly.
5. Serve the soup in bowls and top each with a cheese crouton. Garnish with chopped parsley.

Nutritional Information: Approximately 250 calories per serving, 10 g protein, 30 g carbohydrates, 8 g fat, 4 g fiber, 15 mg cholesterol, 400 mg sodium, 300 mg potassium.

Cream of Mushroom Soup

Yield: 4 servings | Prep time: 15 minutes | Cook time: 25 minutes

Ingredients:

- 500 g fresh mushrooms, cleaned and sliced
- 1 small onion, finely chopped
- 2 cloves garlic, minced
- 1 litre low-sodium vegetable broth
- 200 ml unsweetened almond milk
- 2 tablespoons olive oil
- 2 tablespoons whole wheat flour
- 1 teaspoon dried thyme
- 1/2 teaspoon black pepper
- Salt to taste
- Fresh parsley, chopped (for garnish)

Directions:

1. In a large pot, heat the olive oil over medium heat. Add the onion and garlic and cook until softened, about 3 minutes.
2. Add the mushrooms and cook until they release their moisture and become tender, about 5 minutes.
3. Sprinkle the flour over the mushrooms and stir until well combined. Cook for another 2 minutes.
4. Gradually add the vegetable broth, stirring constantly to prevent lumps from forming. Bring to a simmer.
5. Add the thyme and black pepper. Simmer for about 15 minutes, allowing the flavours to meld.
6. Using a blender or immersion blender, blend half of the soup until smooth. Return the blended soup to the pot and stir in the almond milk. Season with salt to taste.
7. Serve hot, garnished with fresh parsley.

Nutritional Information: Approximately 130 calories per serving, 5 g protein, 15 g carbohydrates, 6 g fat, 3 g fiber, 0 mg cholesterol, 300 mg sodium, 400 mg potassium.

Lemon Orzo and Chicken Soup

Yield: 4 servings | Prep time: 15 minutes | Cook time: 25 minutes

Ingredients:

- 200 g skinless, boneless chicken breast
- 1.5 litres chicken broth (low-sodium)
- 120 g orzo pasta (whole grain)
- 1 small onion, diced
- 2 cloves garlic, minced
- 2 carrots, peeled and diced
- 2 stalks celery, diced
- 1 lemon, zested and juiced
- 1 teaspoon olive oil
- 1 teaspoon dried thyme
- 1 teaspoon dried oregano
- 1/4 teaspoon black pepper
- 2 tablespoons fresh parsley, chopped
- Salt to taste

Directions:

1. In a large pot, heat the olive oil over medium heat. Add the onion, garlic, carrots, and celery. Cook until the vegetables are softened, about 5 minutes.
2. Add the chicken broth, thyme, oregano, and black pepper. Bring to a simmer.
3. Add the chicken breast and simmer for about 15 minutes, or until the chicken is cooked through. Remove the chicken and set it aside to cool slightly. Once it's cool enough to handle, shred it into bite-sized pieces.
4. Add the orzo pasta to the pot and cook for about 8 minutes, or until the pasta is tender.
5. Stir in the shredded chicken, lemon zest, lemon juice, and parsley. Season with salt to taste.
6. Serve hot, garnished with additional fresh parsley if desired.

Nutritional Information: Approximately 240 calories per serving, 20 g protein, 35 g carbohydrates, 3 g fat, 3 g fiber, 40 mg cholesterol, 580 mg sodium, 450 mg potassium.

Slow Cooker Beef and Barley Stew

Yield: 4 servings | Prep time: 15 minutes | Cook time: 240 minutes

Ingredients:

- 500g lean beef stew meat, cut into bite-sized pieces
- 100g pearl barley, rinsed and drained
- 1 onion, chopped
- 2 carrots, chopped
- 2 celery stalks, chopped
- 3 cloves garlic, minced
- 400g canned chopped tomatoes
- 1 litre low-sodium beef broth
- 1 teaspoon dried thyme
- 1 bay leaf
- Salt and pepper to taste
- 2 tablespoons chopped fresh parsley (for garnish)

Directions:

1. In a slow cooker, combine the beef, barley, onion, carrots, celery, garlic, tomatoes, broth, thyme, bay leaf, salt, and pepper. Stir to combine the ingredients.
2. Cover the slow cooker and cook on low for 8 hours or high for 4 hours, until the beef is tender and the barley is cooked through.
3. Discard the bay leaf. Taste and adjust the seasoning as needed.
4. Serve the stew in bowls, garnished with fresh parsley.

Nutritional Information: Approximately 350 calories per serving, 35 g protein, 40 g carbohydrates, 6 g fat, 8 g fiber, 70 mg cholesterol, 550 mg sodium, 800 mg potassium.

Vietnamese Pho with Shirataki Noodles

Yield: 4 servings | Prep time: 15 minutes | Cook time: 30 minutes

Ingredients:

- 1.5 litres beef broth, low sodium
- 1 onion, thinly sliced
- 5 cm piece of fresh ginger, sliced
- 3 cloves garlic, minced
- 2 star anise
- 1 cinnamon stick
- 3 tbsp fish sauce
- 1 tbsp low-sodium soy sauce
- 500 g beef sirloin, thinly sliced
- 200 g shirataki noodles, drained and rinsed
- 2 limes, cut into wedges
- Fresh coriander, chopped (for garnish)
- Fresh basil leaves, chopped (for garnish)
- Fresh mint leaves, chopped (for garnish)
- 1 red chili, thinly sliced (optional, for garnish)
- 100 g bean sprouts (for garnish)
- Sriracha or chili sauce (optional, for serving)

Directions:

1. In a large pot, bring the beef broth to a boil. Add the sliced onion, ginger, garlic, star anise, and cinnamon stick. Reduce the heat to low and let it simmer for about 20 minutes to infuse the flavors.
2. Remove and discard the star anise and cinnamon stick from the broth. Stir in the fish sauce and soy sauce. Bring the broth back to a simmer over medium heat.
3. Divide the shirataki noodles among four serving bowls. Top the noodles with the thinly sliced beef.
4. Ladle the hot broth over the beef and noodles in each bowl. The hot broth will partially cook the beef. Let it sit for a few minutes.
5. Garnish each bowl with lime wedges, fresh herbs, red chili, and bean sprouts. Serve the pho with Sriracha or chili sauce on the side, if desired.

Nutritional Information: Approximately 210 calories per serving, 28 g protein, 10 g carbohydrates, 6 g fat, 3 g fiber, 60 mg cholesterol, 800 mg sodium, 500 mg potassium.

Vegetable Barley Soup
Yield: 4 servings | Prep time: 15 minutes | Cook time: 40 minutes

Ingredients:

- 100 g pearl barley, rinsed and drained
- 1 medium onion, chopped
- 2 cloves garlic, minced
- 2 medium carrots, peeled and chopped
- 2 stalks celery, chopped
- 1 medium courgette, chopped
- 400 g canned diced tomatoes (low sodium)
- 1 litre low-sodium vegetable broth
- 2 tablespoons olive oil
- 1 teaspoon dried basil
- 1 teaspoon dried oregano
- Salt and pepper to taste
- Fresh parsley, chopped (for garnish)

Directions:

1. In a large pot, heat the olive oil over medium heat. Add the onion and garlic and cook until softened, about 3 minutes.
2. Add the carrots, celery, and courgette to the pot. Cook until the vegetables start to soften, about 5 minutes.
3. Stir in the pearl barley, diced tomatoes, vegetable broth, basil, and oregano. Bring the soup to a boil.
4. Reduce heat to low and let simmer for 30 minutes or until the barley is tender and the vegetables are cooked through.
5. Season with salt and pepper to taste. Garnish with chopped parsley before serving.

Nutritional Information: Approximately 200 calories per serving, 6 g protein, 35 g carbohydrates, 5 g fat, 7 g fiber, 0 mg cholesterol, 300 mg sodium, 500 mg potassium.

Seafood Chowder
Yield: 4 servings | Prep time: 20 minutes | Cook time: 25 minutes

Ingredients:

- 2 tablespoons olive oil
- 1 onion, diced
- 2 celery stalks, diced
- 2 cloves garlic, minced
- 1 red bell pepper, diced
- 300g potatoes, diced
- 500ml low-sodium fish or vegetable stock
- 200ml low-fat milk
- 200g mixed seafood (e.g., prawns, mussels, and white fish fillets), cleaned and chopped into bite-sized pieces
- 2 tablespoons fresh parsley, chopped
- 1 teaspoon paprika
- Salt and pepper to taste
- 2 tablespoons chopped fresh dill (for garnish)

Directions:

1. In a large pot, heat the olive oil over medium heat. Add the onion, celery, and garlic and cook until softened, about 5 minutes. Stir in the red bell pepper and cook for an additional 2 minutes.
2. Add the potatoes, stock, milk, paprika, salt, and pepper. Bring the mixture to a boil, then reduce the heat to low and let it simmer until the potatoes are tender, about 15 minutes.
3. Stir in the seafood and cook for an additional 5 minutes, or until the seafood is cooked through. Stir in the parsley.
4. Serve the chowder in bowls, garnished with fresh dill.

Nutritional Information: Approximately 240 calories per serving, 18 g protein, 30 g carbohydrates, 6 g fat, 4 g fiber, 80 mg cholesterol, 500 mg sodium, 650 mg potassium.

Hungarian Goulash with Tender Beef

Yield: 4 servings | Prep time: 15 minutes | Cook time: 2 hours and 15 minutes

Ingredients:

- 500 g beef stewing meat, cut into bite-sized cubes
- 2 tbsp olive oil
- 1 large onion, chopped
- 2 cloves garlic, minced
- 2 tbsp Hungarian paprika
- 1 tsp caraway seeds
- 1/2 tsp ground black pepper
- 1/2 tsp salt
- 1 red bell pepper, chopped

- 400 g canned tomatoes, diced
- 500 ml beef broth, low sodium
- 2 bay leaves
- 2 tbsp tomato paste
- 1 tbsp apple cider vinegar
- 1 tbsp Worcestershire sauce
- 2 large carrots, peeled and diced
- 1 large parsnip, peeled and diced
- Fresh parsley, chopped (for garnish)

Directions:

1. In a large, heavy pot, heat the olive oil over medium-high heat. Add the beef and brown it on all sides, about 5 minutes. Remove the beef and set it aside.
2. Reduce the heat to medium, add the onions and garlic, and sauté until soft, about 3 minutes.
3. Stir in the paprika, caraway seeds, black pepper, and salt. Add the chopped red bell pepper and sauté for another 2 minutes.
4. Return the beef to the pot and add the canned tomatoes, beef broth, bay leaves, tomato paste, vinegar, and Worcestershire sauce. Stir to combine, then bring the mixture to a boil.
5. Reduce the heat to low, cover, and simmer for 2 hours, stirring occasionally, until the beef is tender.
6. Add the carrots and parsnip, and simmer for an additional 15 minutes, or until the vegetables are tender.
7. Adjust the seasoning if needed, remove the bay leaves, and serve the goulash hot, garnished with fresh parsley.

Nutritional Information: Approximately 360 calories per serving, 30 g protein, 25 g carbohydrates, 15 g fat, 6 g fiber, 80 mg cholesterol, 550 mg sodium, 800 mg potassium.

Healthy Side Dishes

Garlic Parmesan Roasted Cauliflower

Yield: 4 servings | Prep time: 10 minutes | Cook time: 25 minutes

Ingredients:

- 1 large cauliflower head (about 600g), cut into florets
- 4 tablespoons olive oil
- 5 cloves garlic, minced
- 50g grated Parmesan cheese
- 1 teaspoon dried thyme
- Salt and black pepper, to taste
- Fresh parsley, chopped (for garnish)

Directions:

1. Preheat your oven to 220°C (425°F). Line a baking sheet with parchment paper.
2. In a large mixing bowl, combine the olive oil, minced garlic, half of the grated Parmesan, thyme, salt, and pepper. Add the cauliflower florets and toss to coat evenly.
3. Spread the cauliflower florets in a single layer on the prepared baking sheet.
4. Roast in the preheated oven for 20-25 minutes, turning the florets halfway through, until they are golden brown and tender.
5. Sprinkle the remaining Parmesan cheese over the cauliflower and return to the oven for an additional 2-3 minutes, until the cheese is melted and slightly crispy.
6. Garnish with chopped parsley and serve.

Nutritional Information: Approximately 200 calories per serving, 7 g protein, 9 g carbohydrates, 16 g fat, 4 g fiber, 10 mg cholesterol, 250 mg sodium, 450 mg potassium.

Lemon and Herb Quinoa Salad

Yield: 4 servings | Prep time: 15 minutes | Cook time: 15 minutes

Ingredients:

- 150g quinoa, rinsed and drained
- 300ml water
- 2 tablespoons olive oil
- Juice and zest of 1 lemon
- 2 tablespoons chopped fresh basil
- 2 tablespoons chopped fresh parsley
- 1 small red onion, finely diced
- 1 medium cucumber, diced
- 150g cherry tomatoes, halved
- 100g feta cheese, crumbled (optional)
- Salt and pepper, to taste

Directions:

1. In a medium saucepan, bring the water to a boil. Add the quinoa and a pinch of salt, then reduce the heat to low. Cover and simmer for 15 minutes or until the quinoa is cooked and the water has been absorbed. Remove from the heat and let it sit for 5 minutes. Fluff the quinoa with a fork and transfer it to a large bowl to cool.
2. In a small bowl, whisk together the olive oil, lemon juice, lemon zest, basil, parsley, salt, and pepper. Set aside.
3. Once the quinoa has cooled, add the red onion, cucumber, cherry tomatoes, and feta cheese (if using) to the bowl. Pour the dressing over the salad and toss until well combined.
4. Serve immediately or refrigerate for later. The salad can be enjoyed cold or at room temperature.

Nutritional Information: Approximately 250 calories per serving, 8 g protein, 30 g carbohydrates, 12 g fat, 4 g fiber, 10 mg cholesterol (if using feta), 200 mg sodium, 350 mg potassium.

Balsamic Glazed Carrots

Yield: 4 servings | Prep time: 10 minutes | Cook time: 15 minutes

Ingredients:

- 500g carrots, peeled and cut into thin rounds
- 1 tablespoon olive oil
- 2 tablespoons balsamic vinegar
- 1 tablespoon honey (or a sugar substitute suitable for diabetics)
- Salt and pepper, to taste
- 2 tablespoons chopped fresh parsley

Directions:

1. In a large non-stick frying pan, heat the olive oil over medium heat. Add the carrots and sauté until they begin to soften, about 5 minutes.
2. In a small bowl, mix together the balsamic vinegar and honey or sugar substitute. Add the mixture to the carrots and continue to sauté, stirring occasionally, until the carrots are tender and the glaze has thickened, about 10 minutes.
3. Season with salt and pepper, then remove from the heat. Transfer the carrots to a serving dish and sprinkle with fresh parsley before serving.

Nutritional Information: Approximately 95 calories per serving, 1 g protein, 17 g carbohydrates, 4 g fat, 3 g fiber, 0 mg cholesterol, 105 mg sodium, 360 mg potassium.

Grilled Zucchini with Feta Cheese

Yield: 4 servings | Prep time: 10 minutes | Cook time: 10 minutes

Ingredients:

- 2 medium-sized zucchinis (about 400g), sliced lengthwise into 1cm thick strips
- 1 tablespoon olive oil
- 1/2 teaspoon dried oregano
- Salt and pepper, to taste
- 100g feta cheese, crumbled
- 2 tablespoons chopped fresh mint

Directions:

1. Preheat the grill to medium-high heat.
2. Brush the zucchini slices with olive oil on both sides. Sprinkle with oregano, salt, and pepper.
3. Place the zucchini slices on the grill and cook for 4-5 minutes on each side, until tender and slightly charred.
4. Transfer the grilled zucchini to a serving platter. Sprinkle with crumbled feta cheese and fresh mint.
5. Serve immediately as a side dish or a light main course.

Nutritional Information: Approximately 105 calories per serving, 4 g protein, 6 g carbohydrates, 8 g fat, 1 g fiber, 15 mg cholesterol, 250 mg sodium, 340 mg potassium.

Steamed Asparagus with Lemon Aioli
Yield: 4 servings | Prep time: 15 minutes | Cook time: 5 minutes

Ingredients:

- 500g fresh asparagus, tough ends trimmed
- Salt, to taste

For the Lemon Aioli:
- 3 tablespoons mayonnaise (low-fat)

- 1 teaspoon lemon zest
- 1 tablespoon lemon juice
- 1 clove garlic, minced
- Salt and pepper, to taste

Directions:

1. Fill a large skillet with about 2 cm of water and bring it to a boil. Add a pinch of salt and the asparagus. Cover and steam the asparagus for about 3-5 minutes, until it is tender but still crisp. Drain the asparagus and transfer it to a serving plate.
2. In a small bowl, combine the mayonnaise, lemon zest, lemon juice, and minced garlic. Season with salt and pepper to taste. Mix until smooth.
3. Drizzle the lemon aioli over the steamed asparagus or serve it on the side as a dipping sauce.
4. Serve immediately as a side dish.

Nutritional Information: Approximately 90 calories per serving, 2 g protein, 6 g carbohydrates, 7 g fat, 2 g fiber, 5 mg cholesterol, 180 mg sodium, 230 mg potassium.

Spinach and Mushroom Sauté
Yield: 4 servings | Prep time: 10 minutes | Cook time: 10 minutes

Ingredients:

- 300g fresh spinach leaves, washed and drained
- 200g mushrooms, sliced
- 1 small onion, finely chopped
- 2 cloves garlic, minced

- 1 tbsp olive oil
- 1/2 tsp dried thyme
- Salt and pepper to taste
- Juice of 1 lemon

Directions:

1. In a large skillet, heat the olive oil over medium heat. Add the chopped onion and sauté for about 2-3 minutes, until it becomes translucent.
2. Add the minced garlic and sliced mushrooms to the skillet. Cook for another 3-4 minutes, until the mushrooms are tender and slightly browned.
3. Add the fresh spinach to the skillet in batches, allowing it to wilt down as you stir. This should take about 2-3 minutes.
4. Season the sautéed mixture with dried thyme, salt, and pepper. Drizzle the lemon juice over the top and stir to combine.
5. Once the spinach is fully wilted and the mixture is heated through, remove the skillet from the heat.
6. Serve the spinach and mushroom sauté as a side dish or as a topping for grilled chicken or fish.

Nutritional Information: Approximately 70 calories per serving, 3g protein, 6g carbohydrates, 4.5g fat, 2g fiber, 0mg cholesterol, 150mg sodium, 450mg potassium.

Greek Tzatziki Cucumber Salad

Yield: 4 servings | Prep time: 15 minutes | Cook time: 0 minutes

Ingredients:

- 2 large cucumbers, peeled and diced
- 200g Greek yogurt (low-fat)
- 2 cloves garlic, minced
- 1 tablespoon fresh dill, chopped
- 1 tablespoon olive oil
- 1 tablespoon lemon juice
- Salt and pepper, to taste
- 1 teaspoon lemon zest
- 50g cherry tomatoes, halved
- 50g Kalamata olives, pitted and halved
- 30g red onion, finely sliced
- 1 tablespoon fresh mint, chopped (optional)

Directions:

1. In a large mixing bowl, combine diced cucumbers, cherry tomatoes, Kalamata olives, and red onion.
2. In a separate bowl, whisk together Greek yogurt, olive oil, lemon juice, minced garlic, dill, and lemon zest. Season with salt and pepper according to preference.
3. Pour the tzatziki dressing over the cucumber mixture and toss well to coat the vegetables evenly.
4. Garnish with fresh mint, if desired. Refrigerate for about 30 minutes before serving to let the flavors meld together.

Nutritional Information: Approximately 110 calories per serving, 4 g protein, 10 g carbohydrates, 6 g fat, 2 g fiber, 5 mg cholesterol, 150 mg sodium, 300 mg potassium.

Garlic Butter Green Beans

Yield: 4 servings | Prep time: 10 minutes | Cook time: 10 minutes

Ingredients:

- 400g green beans, trimmed
- 3 tablespoons unsalted butter
- 4 cloves garlic, minced
- Salt and pepper, to taste
- Zest of 1 lemon
- 2 tablespoons lemon juice
- 2 tablespoons fresh parsley, chopped

Directions:

1. Bring a large pot of salted water to a boil. Add green beans and blanch for 3-4 minutes, until just tender but still crisp. Drain the beans and plunge them into ice water to stop the cooking process. Drain again.
2. In a large skillet, melt the butter over medium heat. Add the minced garlic and sauté until fragrant, about 1-2 minutes.
3. Add the blanched green beans to the skillet. Toss to coat the beans in the garlic butter. Season with salt and pepper.
4. Cook for 2-3 minutes, until the beans are heated through. Stir in the lemon zest and juice.
5. Remove from heat and transfer to a serving dish. Garnish with fresh parsley.

Nutritional Information: Approximately 110 calories per serving, 2 g protein, 8 g carbohydrates, 8 g fat, 3 g fiber, 23 mg cholesterol, 120 mg sodium, 250 mg potassium.

Roasted Sweet Potato and Beet Salad

Yield: 4 servings | Prep time: 15 minutes | Cook time: 40 minutes

Ingredients:

- 2 large sweet potatoes (about 400g), peeled and cut into bite-sized pieces
- 2 medium beets (about 300g), peeled and cut into bite-sized pieces
- 3 tablespoons olive oil
- Salt and pepper, to taste
- 4 cups (120g) mixed salad greens
- 1/4 cup (30g) feta cheese, crumbled
- 1/4 cup (30g) walnuts, toasted and chopped
- 2 tablespoons balsamic vinegar
- 1 teaspoon Dijon mustard

Directions:

1. Preheat your oven to 200°C (400°F). Place the sweet potatoes and beets on a baking sheet, drizzle with 2 tablespoons of olive oil, and season with salt and pepper. Toss to coat the vegetables evenly and spread them out in a single layer.
2. Roast in the preheated oven for 35-40 minutes, or until the vegetables are tender and slightly caramelized, stirring once or twice during roasting.
3. In a large salad bowl, combine the roasted vegetables with the salad greens, feta cheese, and walnuts.
4. In a small bowl, whisk together the balsamic vinegar, Dijon mustard, and the remaining tablespoon of olive oil. Season with salt and pepper to taste. Drizzle the dressing over the salad and toss to coat.

Nutritional Information: Approximately 275 calories per serving, 6 g protein, 34 g carbohydrates, 14 g fat, 6 g fiber, 8 mg cholesterol, 380 mg sodium, 650 mg potassium.

Mediterranean Orzo Salad

Yield: 4 servings | Prep time: 15 minutes | Cook time: 10 minutes

Ingredients:

- 200g orzo pasta
- 2 tablespoons olive oil
- 1 small red onion, finely chopped
- 1 small red bell pepper, diced
- 1 small yellow bell pepper, diced
- 1 small cucumber, diced
- 100g cherry tomatoes, halved
- 50g feta cheese, crumbled
- 30g Kalamata olives, pitted and sliced
- 2 tablespoons fresh parsley, chopped
- 2 tablespoons fresh basil, chopped
- 1 tablespoon fresh lemon juice
- 1 teaspoon balsamic vinegar
- Salt and pepper, to taste

Directions:

1. Cook the orzo according to package instructions until al dente. Drain and rinse under cold water to stop the cooking process. Transfer to a large salad bowl.
2. Add the red onion, red and yellow bell peppers, cucumber, cherry tomatoes, feta cheese, olives, parsley, and basil to the orzo.
3. In a small bowl, whisk together the olive oil, lemon juice, balsamic vinegar, salt, and pepper. Drizzle the dressing over the salad and toss to combine.
4. Chill the salad in the refrigerator for at least 30 minutes before serving.

Nutritional Information: Approximately 320 calories per serving, 9 g protein, 47 g carbohydrates, 11 g fat, 3 g fiber, 8 mg cholesterol, 380 mg sodium, 320 mg potassium.

Spicy Kimchi Slaw

Yield: 4 servings | Prep time: 15 minutes | Cook time: 0 minutes

Ingredients:

- 200g shredded red cabbage
- 200g shredded green cabbage
- 1 medium carrot, grated
- 4 spring onions, thinly sliced
- 150g kimchi, chopped
- 2 tablespoons rice vinegar
- 1 tablespoon soy sauce
- 1 tablespoon sesame oil
- 1 tablespoon gochujang (Korean red chili paste)
- 1 tablespoon toasted sesame seeds
- 1 small red chili, thinly sliced (optional)
- Salt, to taste

Directions:

1. In a large bowl, combine the shredded red and green cabbage, grated carrot, sliced spring onions, and chopped kimchi.
2. In a small bowl, whisk together the rice vinegar, soy sauce, sesame oil, gochujang, and a pinch of salt until well combined.
3. Pour the dressing over the slaw and toss until all ingredients are well coated.
4. Garnish with toasted sesame seeds and sliced red chili, if desired.
5. Serve immediately or refrigerate for at least 30 minutes to allow the flavors to meld.

Nutritional Information: Approximately 105 calories per serving, 4 g protein, 15 g carbohydrates, 4 g fat, 3 g fiber, 0 mg cholesterol, 580 mg sodium, 280 mg potassium.

Lemon Garlic Broccoli

Yield: 4 servings | Prep time: 10 minutes | Cook time: 10 minutes

Ingredients:

- 500g broccoli florets
- 3 tablespoons olive oil
- 4 cloves garlic, minced
- Zest and juice of 1 lemon
- Salt, to taste
- Black pepper, to taste
- 1 tablespoon chopped fresh parsley (optional)

Directions:

1. In a large pot of boiling salted water, blanch the broccoli florets for 3 minutes. Drain and set aside.
2. In a large skillet, heat the olive oil over medium heat. Add the minced garlic and sauté until fragrant, about 1 minute.
3. Add the blanched broccoli to the skillet and toss to coat in the garlic and oil.
4. Stir in the lemon zest, lemon juice, salt, and black pepper. Cook for an additional 2-3 minutes, or until the broccoli is tender but still slightly crisp.
5. Garnish with chopped parsley if desired. Serve hot.

Nutritional Information: Approximately 110 calories per serving, 4 g protein, 11 g carbohydrates, 7 g fat, 4 g fiber, 0 mg cholesterol, 30 mg sodium, 450 mg potassium.

Spaghetti Squash with Parmesan

Yield: 4 servings | Prep time: 10 minutes | Cook time: 40 minutes

Ingredients:

- 1 large spaghetti squash (about 1.5 kg)
- 2 tablespoons olive oil
- 2 cloves garlic, minced
- 60g grated Parmesan cheese
- Salt, to taste
- Black pepper, to taste
- 2 tablespoons chopped fresh parsley (optional)

Directions:

1. Preheat your oven to 190°C (375°F).
2. Cut the spaghetti squash in half lengthwise and scoop out the seeds and fibrous strands. Brush the inside of each half with 1 tablespoon of olive oil.
3. Place the squash halves cut-side down on a baking sheet lined with parchment paper and bake for 35-40 minutes, or until the flesh is tender and easily shredded with a fork.
4. Once the squash is done baking, let it cool for a few minutes. Then, use a fork to scrape the flesh into spaghetti-like strands.
5. In a large skillet, heat the remaining 1 tablespoon of olive oil over medium heat. Add the minced garlic and sauté until fragrant, about 1 minute.
6. Add the shredded spaghetti squash to the skillet and toss to coat with the garlic and oil. Stir in the grated Parmesan cheese and season with salt and black pepper to taste.
7. Garnish with chopped parsley if desired. Serve hot.

Nutritional Information: Approximately 170 calories per serving, 6 g protein, 19 g carbohydrates, 9 g fat, 3.5 g fiber, 10 mg cholesterol, 290 mg sodium, 270 mg potassium.

Baked Brussels Sprouts with Bacon

Yield: 4 servings | Prep time: 15 minutes | Cook time: 25 minutes

Ingredients:

- 500g Brussels sprouts, trimmed and halved
- 100g bacon, chopped
- 2 tablespoons olive oil
- Salt, to taste
- Black pepper, to taste
- 2 tablespoons balsamic vinegar
- 1 tablespoon whole grain mustard

Directions:

1. Preheat your oven to 200°C (400°F). In a large baking dish, toss the Brussels sprouts with the chopped bacon, olive oil, salt, and black pepper. Spread the mixture out in an even layer.
2. Roast the Brussels sprouts and bacon in the preheated oven for about 20 minutes, or until the sprouts are tender and the bacon is crispy, stirring halfway through the cooking time.
3. In a small bowl, whisk together the balsamic vinegar and whole grain mustard. Drizzle the mixture over the roasted Brussels sprouts and bacon, and toss to combine.
4. Serve the baked Brussels sprouts and bacon hot, as a side dish or as a light meal.

Nutritional Information: Approximately 210 calories per serving, 8 g protein, 12 g carbohydrates, 15 g fat, 4 g fiber, 20 mg cholesterol, 480 mg sodium, 440 mg potassium.

Creamy Avocado and Tomato Salad

Yield: 4 servings | Prep time: 10 minutes | Cook time: 0 minutes

Ingredients:

- 2 ripe avocados, peeled, pitted, and diced
- 300g cherry tomatoes, halved
- 1 small red onion, finely sliced
- 1 garlic clove, minced
- 60ml Greek yogurt (full fat)
- 2 tablespoons lemon juice
- 2 tablespoons olive oil
- Salt and black pepper, to taste
- 2 tablespoons fresh basil, chopped

Directions:

1. In a large bowl, combine the diced avocados, halved cherry tomatoes, and sliced red onion.
2. In a small bowl, whisk together the minced garlic, Greek yogurt, lemon juice, olive oil, salt, and black pepper. Adjust the seasoning to taste.
3. Pour the dressing over the avocado and tomato mixture, and gently toss to coat.
4. Sprinkle with chopped fresh basil and serve immediately.

Nutritional Information: Approximately 230 calories per serving, 4 g protein, 15 g carbohydrates, 18 g fat, 7 g fiber, 2 mg cholesterol, 80 mg sodium, 650 mg potassium.

Miso Glazed Eggplant

Yield: 4 servings | Prep time: 10 minutes | Cook time: 20 minutes

Ingredients:

- 2 medium eggplants (about 600g)
- 2 tablespoons miso paste
- 1 tablespoon mirin
- 1 tablespoon sake
- 1 tablespoon soy sauce
- 1 tablespoon sesame oil
- 1 tablespoon grated fresh ginger
- 2 cloves garlic, minced
- 2 spring onions, thinly sliced
- 1 tablespoon sesame seeds
- Fresh coriander leaves, for garnish

Directions:

1. Preheat the oven to 220°C (425°F).
2. Cut the eggplants in half lengthwise. Score the flesh of each eggplant half with a sharp knife in a crisscross pattern.
3. In a small bowl, whisk together the miso paste, mirin, sake, soy sauce, sesame oil, grated ginger, and minced garlic.
4. Brush the miso mixture onto the cut side of each eggplant half, making sure to get it into the scored lines.
5. Place the eggplant halves, skin side down, on a baking sheet lined with parchment paper.
6. Roast the eggplant in the preheated oven for 20 minutes, or until the flesh is tender and the glaze is caramelized.
7. Remove from the oven and sprinkle with sliced spring onions and sesame seeds. Garnish with fresh coriander leaves.
8. Serve warm.

Nutritional Information: Approximately 118 calories per serving, 3 g protein, 19 g carbohydrates, 4 g fat, 6 g fiber, 0 mg cholesterol, 540 mg sodium, 467 mg potassium.

Garlic and Herb Sautéed Spinach

Yield: 4 servings | Prep time: 5 minutes | Cook time: 5 minutes

Ingredients:

- 450g fresh spinach, washed and drained
- 2 tablespoons olive oil
- 4 cloves garlic, minced
- 1 teaspoon dried oregano
- 1 teaspoon dried basil
- Salt and black pepper, to taste
- 1 tablespoon fresh lemon juice

Directions:

1. Heat olive oil in a large skillet over medium heat. Add the minced garlic and sauté until fragrant, about 1 minute.
2. Add the spinach to the skillet, in batches if necessary, and stir until wilted, about 2-3 minutes.
3. Stir in the dried oregano and dried basil, and season with salt and black pepper to taste.
4. Remove from heat and drizzle with fresh lemon juice.
5. Serve immediately.

Nutritional Information: Approximately 85 calories per serving, 2 g protein, 6 g carbohydrates, 6 g fat, 2 g fiber, 0 mg cholesterol, 120 mg sodium, 480 mg potassium.

Zesty Lemon and Dill Coleslaw

Yield: 4 servings | Prep time: 15 minutes | Cook time: 0 minutes

Ingredients:

- 400g white cabbage, shredded
- 100g carrots, grated
- 4 green onions, thinly sliced
- 60g mayonnaise
- 2 tablespoons fresh lemon juice
- 1 tablespoon white wine vinegar
- 2 tablespoons fresh dill, chopped
- Salt and black pepper, to taste
- Lemon zest, for garnish

Directions:

1. In a large bowl, combine the shredded cabbage, grated carrots, and sliced green onions.
2. In a separate bowl, whisk together the mayonnaise, fresh lemon juice, white wine vinegar, and chopped dill. Season with salt and black pepper to taste.
3. Pour the dressing over the cabbage mixture and toss to combine. Ensure all ingredients are well-coated with the dressing.
4. Cover the bowl with plastic wrap and refrigerate for at least 30 minutes, allowing the flavors to meld.
5. Serve chilled, garnished with lemon zest.

Nutritional Information: Approximately 145 calories per serving, 1 g protein, 12 g carbohydrates, 11 g fat, 3 g fiber, 8 mg cholesterol, 205 mg sodium, 265 mg potassium.

Warm Potato Salad with Dijon Mustard Dressing
Yield: 4 servings | Prep time: 15 minutes | Cook time: 25 minutes

Ingredients:

- 600g new potatoes
- 1 tablespoon olive oil
- 2 tablespoons Dijon mustard
- 2 tablespoons white wine vinegar
- 2 tablespoons chopped fresh parsley
- 1 small red onion, finely diced
- 1 clove garlic, minced
- Salt and pepper, to taste
- 2 spring onions, thinly sliced
- 1 tablespoon capers, drained

Directions:

1. Place the potatoes in a large pot and cover with cold water. Add a pinch of salt. Bring to a boil and then reduce the heat to medium. Simmer for 20-25 minutes or until the potatoes are tender when pierced with a fork. Drain and let cool slightly.
2. In a small bowl, whisk together the olive oil, Dijon mustard, white wine vinegar, parsley, red onion, garlic, salt, and pepper.
3. Cut the warm potatoes into quarters and place them in a large bowl
4. Pour the Dijon mustard dressing over the potatoes. Add the spring onions and capers. Toss gently to coat the potatoes with the dressing.
5. Serve the potato salad warm.

Nutritional Information: Approximately 165 calories per serving, 3 g protein, 33 g carbohydrates, 4 g fat, 4 g fiber, 0 mg cholesterol, 270 mg sodium, 775 mg potassium.

Vibrant Vegetarian Dishes

Zucchini Noodles with Avocado Pesto
Yield: 4 servings | Prep time: 15 minutes | Cook time: 5 minutes

Ingredients:

- 4 medium zucchinis, spiralized into noodles
- 2 ripe avocados
- 2 cloves garlic, minced
- 30g fresh basil leaves
- 2 tablespoons lemon juice
- 60ml olive oil
- Salt and pepper, to taste
- 30g pine nuts, toasted
- 30g grated Parmesan cheese
- Cherry tomatoes, for garnish

Directions:

1. In a large pot, bring water to a boil. Add the zucchini noodles and cook for 2-3 minutes, until tender but not mushy. Drain and set aside.
2. In a food processor, combine the avocados, garlic, basil, lemon juice, olive oil, salt, and pepper. Process until smooth and creamy.
3. In a large bowl, toss the zucchini noodles with the avocado pesto. Add the pine nuts and Parmesan cheese, and toss gently to combine.
4. Serve immediately, garnished with cherry tomatoes.

Nutritional Information: Approximately 325 calories per serving, 7 g protein, 18 g carbohydrates, 27 g fat, 8 g fiber, 4 mg cholesterol, 180 mg sodium, 750 mg potassium.

Eggplant and Chickpea Curry
Yield: 4 servings | Prep time: 15 minutes | Cook time: 35 minutes

Ingredients:

- 2 medium eggplants, diced
- 1 tablespoon olive oil
- 1 large onion, chopped
- 3 cloves garlic, minced
- 1 tablespoon ginger, minced
- 2 tablespoons curry powder
- 1 teaspoon ground turmeric
- 1 teaspoon ground cumin
- 1/2 teaspoon chili powder
- 1 (400g) can chickpeas, drained and rinsed
- 1 (400g) can diced tomatoes
- 1 (400g) can light coconut milk
- Salt and pepper, to taste
- Fresh coriander, chopped for garnish

Directions:

1. In a large skillet, heat the olive oil over medium heat. Add the onions, garlic, and ginger and sauté until softened, about 5 minutes.
2. Add the curry powder, turmeric, cumin, and chili powder to the skillet and sauté for another 2 minutes until fragrant.
3. Stir in the diced eggplants and sauté until they start to soften, about 5 minutes.
4. Add the chickpeas, diced tomatoes (with their juice), and coconut milk to the skillet. Bring to a simmer, then reduce the heat to low, cover, and simmer for 25 minutes, stirring occasionally.
5. Season the curry with salt and pepper to taste. Garnish with fresh coriander before serving.

Nutritional Information: Approximately 240 calories per serving, 9 g protein, 30 g carbohydrates, 11 g fat, 11 g fiber, 0 mg cholesterol, 700 mg sodium, 900 mg potassium.

Stuffed Acorn Squash with Wild Rice and Cranberries

Yield: 4 servings | Prep time: 20 minutes | Cook time: 60 minutes

Ingredients:

- 2 acorn squash, halved and seeds removed
- 2 tablespoons olive oil
- Salt and pepper, to taste
- 150g wild rice
- 500ml vegetable broth
- 1 small onion, chopped
- 2 cloves garlic, minced
- 100g dried cranberries
- 50g chopped pecans
- 2 tablespoons chopped fresh parsley
- 1 tablespoon balsamic vinegar

Directions:

1. Preheat your oven to 200°C. Brush the inside of the acorn squash with 1 tablespoon of the olive oil and season with salt and pepper. Place the squash cut side down on a baking tray and bake for 40-45 minutes, until the flesh is tender.
2. While the squash is baking, cook the wild rice according to the package instructions using the vegetable broth.
3. In a large skillet, heat the remaining tablespoon of olive oil over medium heat. Add the onion and garlic and sauté for 5-7 minutes, until the onion is soft and translucent. Stir in the cooked wild rice, dried cranberries, pecans, parsley, and balsamic vinegar.
4. Fill each acorn squash half with the wild rice mixture. Return the squash to the oven for 10-15 minutes, until the filling is heated through.

Nutritional Information: Approximately 330 calories per serving, 7 g protein, 55 g carbohydrates, 11 g fat, 6 g fiber, 0 mg cholesterol, 320 mg sodium, 800 mg potassium.

Spinach and Ricotta Stuffed Mushrooms

Yield: 4 servings | Prep time: 15 minutes | Cook time: 25 minutes

Ingredients:

- 8 large portobello mushrooms, stems removed and cleaned
- 200g spinach, washed and roughly chopped
- 150g ricotta cheese
- 2 cloves garlic, minced
- 50g grated Parmesan cheese
- 1 tablespoon olive oil
- Salt and pepper, to taste
- 1/4 teaspoon nutmeg
- 1/4 teaspoon crushed red pepper flakes (optional)

Directions:

1. Preheat the oven to 190°C (375°F). Grease a baking dish with olive oil.
2. Heat the olive oil in a skillet over medium heat. Add the garlic and sauté until fragrant, about 1 minute.
3. Add the spinach to the skillet and sauté until wilted, about 3 minutes. Remove from heat and let it cool slightly.
4. In a medium bowl, combine the ricotta cheese, sautéed spinach, half of the Parmesan cheese, nutmeg, and red pepper flakes (if using). Season with salt and pepper to taste.
5. Stuff each mushroom cap with the spinach and ricotta mixture, then sprinkle the remaining Parmesan cheese on top.
6. Place the stuffed mushrooms in the prepared baking dish. Bake for 20 minutes, or until the mushrooms are tender and the cheese is melted and lightly golden brown.

Nutritional Information: Approximately 140 calories per serving, 8 g protein, 6 g carbohydrates, 10 g fat, 2 g fiber, 25 mg cholesterol, 320 mg sodium, 500 mg potassium.

Butternut Squash and Kale Risotto
Yield: 4 servings | Prep time: 15 minutes | Cook time: 35 minutes

Ingredients:

- 200g arborio rice
- 500g butternut squash, peeled, seeded and diced
- 150g kale, stemmed and chopped
- 1 onion, diced
- 2 cloves garlic, minced
- 1 liter vegetable broth
- 60ml white wine (optional)
- 30g Parmesan cheese, grated
- 1 tablespoon olive oil
- Salt and pepper, to taste
- 1/4 teaspoon ground nutmeg

Directions:

1. Heat the olive oil in a large skillet over medium heat. Add the onion and sauté until translucent, about 5 minutes.
2. Add the garlic and sauté for an additional minute until fragrant.
3. Stir in the rice and sauté for 2 minutes until it begins to toast slightly.
4. If using wine, add it to the skillet and stir until it evaporates. If not using wine, proceed to the next step.
5. Gradually add the vegetable broth, one cup at a time, stirring frequently and allowing the liquid to be absorbed before adding the next cup.
6. After the first cup of broth is absorbed, add the butternut squash. Continue adding broth until the rice is creamy and the squash is tender, about 25 minutes.
7. Stir in the kale and cook until wilted, about 2 minutes.
8. Remove from heat and stir in the Parmesan cheese, nutmeg, salt, and pepper.

Nutritional Information: Approximately 300 calories per serving, 8 g protein, 58 g carbohydrates, 6 g fat, 4 g fiber, 5 mg cholesterol, 700 mg sodium, 600 mg potassium.

Mediterranean Lentil and Feta Salad
Yield: 4 servings | Prep time: 15 minutes | Cook time: 20 minutes

Ingredients:

- 200g dried green lentils
- 100g feta cheese, crumbled
- 1 red onion, diced
- 1 red bell pepper, diced
- 1 cucumber, diced
- 150g cherry tomatoes, halved
- 50g kalamata olives, pitted and halved
- 2 cloves garlic, minced
- 4 tablespoons olive oil
- 2 tablespoons red wine vinegar
- 1 teaspoon dried oregano
- Salt and pepper, to taste
- 2 tablespoons fresh parsley, chopped

Directions:

1. Rinse the lentils under cold water and then place them in a large saucepan with plenty of water. Bring to a boil, then reduce the heat to a simmer and cook for 20 minutes or until the lentils are tender but not mushy. Drain and let them cool.
2. In a large bowl, combine the cooled lentils with the red onion, red bell pepper, cucumber, cherry tomatoes, olives, and feta cheese.
3. In a small bowl, whisk together the olive oil, red wine vinegar, garlic, oregano, salt, and pepper. Pour the dressing over the salad and toss to combine.
4. Chill the salad in the refrigerator for at least 30 minutes to let the flavors meld together. Serve the salad garnished with fresh parsley.

Nutritional Information: Approximately 340 calories per serving, 14 g protein, 30 g carbohydrates, 18 g fat, 12 g fiber, 15 mg cholesterol, 560 mg sodium, 610 mg potassium.

Hearty Vegetable and Bean Chili

Yield: 6 servings | Prep time: 15 minutes | Cook time: 45 minutes

Ingredients:

- 2 tablespoons olive oil
- 1 large onion, chopped
- 2 carrots, chopped
- 2 stalks celery, chopped
- 2 bell peppers (1 red, 1 green), chopped
- 3 cloves garlic, minced
- 1 zucchini, chopped
- 1 teaspoon chili powder
- 1 teaspoon ground cumin
- 1/2 teaspoon smoked paprika
- 400g canned diced tomatoes
- 400g canned black beans, drained and rinsed
- 400g canned kidney beans, drained and rinsed
- 250ml vegetable stock
- Salt and pepper, to taste
- Fresh coriander leaves, for garnish

Directions:

1. In a large saucepan or Dutch oven, heat the olive oil over medium heat. Add the onions, carrots, celery, and bell peppers. Sauté the vegetables until the onions are translucent, about 5 minutes.
2. Add the garlic, zucchini, chili powder, cumin, and smoked paprika to the pot. Sauté for an additional 2 minutes until the spices are fragrant.
3. Stir in the diced tomatoes, black beans, kidney beans, and vegetable stock. Season with salt and pepper. Bring the chili to a simmer, then reduce the heat to low and let it cook for about 30 minutes, stirring occasionally.
4. Serve the chili in bowls, garnished with fresh coriander leaves.

Nutritional Information: Approximately 275 calories per serving, 14 g protein, 45 g carbohydrates, 5 g fat, 13 g fiber, 0 mg cholesterol, 650 mg sodium, 960 mg potassium.

Cauliflower Steaks with Chimichurri

Yield: 4 servings | Prep time: 10 minutes | Cook time: 25 minutes

Ingredients:

- 1 large cauliflower (about 1 kg)
- 3 tablespoons olive oil
- Salt and pepper to taste
- For the Chimichurri:
- 50g fresh parsley, finely chopped
- 25g fresh coriander, finely chopped
- 2 cloves garlic, minced
- 1 red chili, finely chopped (optional)
- 120 ml olive oil
- 2 tablespoons red wine vinegar
- Salt and pepper to taste

Directions:

1. Preheat your oven to 220°C (200°C fan-assisted). Line a baking sheet with parchment paper.
2. Remove the leaves and stem from the cauliflower, then cut the cauliflower into 2 cm thick steaks. You should get about 4 steaks from a large cauliflower.
3. Place the cauliflower steaks on the baking sheet, brush with olive oil, and season with salt and pepper. Roast in the oven for 20-25 minutes or until tender and golden brown.
4. While the cauliflower is roasting, make the chimichurri. In a small bowl, combine the parsley, coriander, garlic, chili (if using), olive oil, and red wine vinegar. Season with salt and pepper to taste. Stir well.
5. Once the cauliflower steaks are cooked, remove from the oven and transfer to serving plates. Drizzle with chimichurri and serve immediately.

Nutritional Information: Approximately 290 calories per serving, 4 g protein, 14 g carbohydrates, 25 g fat, 5 g fiber, 0 mg cholesterol, 100 mg sodium, 500 mg potassium.

Grilled Portobello Mushrooms with Balsamic Glaze
Yield: 4 servings | Prep time: 15 minutes | Cook time: 10 minutes

Ingredients:

- 4 large portobello mushrooms, cleaned and stems removed
- 2 tablespoons olive oil
- 2 tablespoons balsamic vinegar
- 1 teaspoon honey
- 2 cloves garlic, minced
- 1 teaspoon dried thyme
- Salt and pepper, to taste
- Fresh parsley, chopped (for garnish)

Directions:

1. In a small bowl, whisk together the olive oil, balsamic vinegar, honey, garlic, thyme, salt, and pepper. This will be your marinade and glaze.
2. Brush the mushrooms with the marinade, making sure to coat them well. Let them marinate for 10 minutes.
3. Preheat your grill or griddle pan to medium-high heat. Place the mushrooms on the grill, cap-side down. Grill for 4-5 minutes on each side, or until they are tender and have grill marks.
4. Once cooked, remove the mushrooms from the grill and place them on a serving plate. Drizzle any remaining marinade over the top as a glaze.
5. Garnish with chopped parsley and serve.

Nutritional Information: Approximately 100 calories per serving, 2 g protein, 10 g carbohydrates, 7 g fat, 2 g fiber, 0 mg cholesterol, 150 mg sodium, 300 mg potassium.

Thai Basil and Tofu Stir Fry
Yield: 4 servings | Prep time: 15 minutes | Cook time: 10 minutes

Ingredients:

- 400g firm tofu, drained and cubed
- 1 tablespoon vegetable oil
- 2 cloves garlic, minced
- 1 red chili, deseeded and finely chopped
- 1 red bell pepper, sliced
- 1 yellow bell pepper, sliced
- 200g snow peas, trimmed
- 200g mushrooms, sliced
- 1 tablespoon soy sauce
- 1 tablespoon oyster sauce (vegetarian version available)
- 1 teaspoon brown sugar
- 1 tablespoon water
- 40g fresh Thai basil leaves

Directions:

1. Press the tofu to remove excess water. Cut into 2 cm cubes.
2. Heat oil in a large wok or skillet over medium-high heat. Add the tofu and cook until golden brown on all sides, about 4-5 minutes. Remove tofu from the wok and set aside.
3. In the same wok, add the garlic and chili. Stir-fry for 1 minute until fragrant. Add the bell peppers, snow peas, and mushrooms. Stir-fry for 3-4 minutes until the vegetables are tender-crisp.
4. In a small bowl, mix together the soy sauce, oyster sauce, brown sugar, and water. Pour this sauce over the vegetables and add the cooked tofu. Stir well to combine.
5. Add the Thai basil leaves and toss until the leaves are wilted.
6. Serve immediately over rice or noodles.

Nutritional Information: Approximately 220 calories per serving, 17 g protein, 15 g carbohydrates, 11 g fat, 4 g fiber, 0 mg cholesterol, 350 mg sodium, 540 mg potassium.

Mushroom and Goat Cheese Tart

Yield: 6 servings | Prep time: 15 minutes | Cook time: 35 minutes

Ingredients:

- 150g whole wheat flour
- 75g cold unsalted butter, cubed
- 4 tablespoons cold water
- 2 tablespoons olive oil
- 2 small onions, finely chopped
- 4 cloves garlic, minced
- 300g mushrooms (mixed varieties such as button, chestnut, and shiitake), sliced

- 150g goat cheese, crumbled
- 2 large eggs
- 100ml skim milk
- 1 tablespoon chopped fresh thyme
- Salt and pepper, to taste
- Fresh parsley, for garnish

Directions:

1. In a large bowl, combine the flour and butter. Use your fingertips to rub the butter into the flour until the mixture resembles coarse breadcrumbs. Gradually add the cold water and mix until the dough comes together. Form the dough into a disc, wrap in plastic wrap, and chill in the refrigerator for at least 30 minutes.
2. Preheat the oven to 180°C (350°F). Roll out the chilled dough and fit it into a 23cm (9-inch) tart pan. Trim any excess dough, and prick the bottom with a fork. Bake the crust for 10 minutes, until lightly golden.
3. In a large skillet, heat the olive oil over medium heat. Add the onions and garlic, and sauté until softened, about 5 minutes. Add the mushrooms and cook until they release their juices and become tender. Season with salt and pepper, and set aside.
4. In a bowl, whisk together the eggs, milk, and thyme. Season with salt and pepper. Spread the mushroom mixture evenly over the tart crust, and sprinkle the goat cheese on top. Pour the egg mixture over the filling.
5. Bake the tart for 25 minutes, or until the filling is set and the top is lightly browned. Allow the tart to cool for a few minutes before slicing. Garnish with fresh parsley.

Nutritional Information: Approximately 280 calories per serving, 11 g protein, 22 g carbohydrates, 17 g fat, 3 g fiber, 85 mg cholesterol, 350 mg sodium, 310 mg potassium.

Artichoke and Spinach Stuffed Pasta Shells

Yield: 4 servings | Prep time: 30 minutes | Cook time: 25 minutes

Ingredients:

- 16 large pasta shells (about 100g)
- 200g canned artichoke hearts, drained and chopped
- 200g fresh spinach, chopped
- 200g ricotta cheese
- 50g grated Parmesan cheese
- 2 cloves garlic, minced
- 1 teaspoon olive oil
- Salt and pepper, to taste
- 400g canned chopped tomatoes
- 1 teaspoon dried basil
- 1 teaspoon dried oregano
- 100g grated mozzarella cheese

Directions:

1. Preheat your oven to 200°C. Cook the pasta shells according to the package instructions until al dente. Drain and set aside.
2. In a large frying pan, heat the olive oil over medium heat. Add the garlic and sauté for 1 minute. Add the spinach and cook until wilted. Remove from heat and let it cool.
3. In a mixing bowl, combine the ricotta cheese, Parmesan cheese, artichoke hearts, and cooked spinach. Season with salt and pepper. Mix until well combined.
4. Stuff each pasta shell with the artichoke and spinach mixture. Arrange the stuffed shells in a baking dish.
5. In a saucepan, combine the canned tomatoes, basil, and oregano. Bring to a simmer over medium heat. Cook for 5 minutes, stirring occasionally.
6. Pour the tomato sauce over the stuffed shells. Sprinkle the grated mozzarella cheese on top.
7. Cover the baking dish with foil and bake for 20 minutes. Remove the foil and bake for an additional 5 minutes, or until the cheese is melted and bubbly.

Nutritional Information: Approximately 310 calories per serving, 18 g protein, 30 g carbohydrates, 14 g fat, 6 g fiber, 40 mg cholesterol, 670 mg sodium, 720 mg potassium.

Baked Eggplant Parmesan
Yield: 4 servings | Prep time: 20 minutes | Cook time: 40 minutes

Ingredients:

- 2 large eggplants, sliced into 1 cm thick rounds
- Salt, to taste
- 2 eggs
- 100g whole wheat breadcrumbs
- 2 teaspoons Italian seasoning
- 50g grated Parmesan cheese
- 400g canned chopped tomatoes
- 2 cloves garlic, minced
- 1 teaspoon olive oil
- 200g grated mozzarella cheese
- 2 tablespoons fresh basil leaves, chopped

Directions:

1. Preheat your oven to 200°C. Line a baking sheet with parchment paper.
2. Sprinkle the eggplant slices with salt on both sides and let them sit for 15 minutes. Rinse the slices under cold water and pat them dry with paper towels.
3. In a shallow bowl, beat the eggs. In another shallow bowl, mix the breadcrumbs, Italian seasoning, and Parmesan cheese. Dip each eggplant slice in the egg and then in the breadcrumb mixture, making sure to coat each slice evenly. Place the coated slices on the prepared baking sheet.
4. Bake the eggplant slices for 20 minutes, turning them over halfway through the cooking time, until they are golden brown.
5. In a saucepan, heat the olive oil over medium heat. Add the garlic and sauté for 1 minute. Add the canned tomatoes and bring to a simmer. Cook for 10 minutes, stirring occasionally.
6. In a baking dish, layer the baked eggplant slices, tomato sauce, and mozzarella cheese. Repeat the layers until all the ingredients are used up, finishing with a layer of mozzarella cheese on top.
7. Bake the dish for 20 minutes, or until the cheese is melted and bubbly. Garnish with fresh basil before serving.

Nutritional Information: Approximately 320 calories per serving, 17 g protein, 30 g carbohydrates, 15 g fat, 9 g fiber, 60 mg cholesterol, 670 mg sodium, 800 mg potassium.

Roasted Vegetable and Couscous Salad

Yield: 4 servings | Prep time: 15 minutes | Cook time: 25 minutes

Ingredients:

- 200g whole wheat couscous
- 1 small aubergine, chopped into bite-sized pieces
- 1 small courgette, chopped into bite-sized pieces
- 1 red bell pepper, chopped into bite-sized pieces
- 1 yellow bell pepper, chopped into bite-sized pieces
- 1 red onion, chopped into bite-sized pieces
- 3 tablespoons olive oil
- 2 tablespoons balsamic vinegar
- 1 teaspoon dried oregano
- Salt and pepper, to taste
- 100g baby spinach
- 50g feta cheese, crumbled
- 2 tablespoons chopped fresh basil

Directions:

1. Preheat your oven to 200°C. In a large bowl, toss the aubergine, courgette, bell peppers, and onion with 2 tablespoons of olive oil, balsamic vinegar, oregano, salt, and pepper. Spread the vegetables out on a baking tray and roast in the oven for 20-25 minutes, stirring halfway through, until the vegetables are tender and slightly caramelized.
2. While the vegetables are roasting, prepare the couscous according to the package instructions. Fluff the couscous with a fork, then let it cool slightly.
3. In a large bowl, combine the roasted vegetables, cooked couscous, and baby spinach. Drizzle the remaining 1 tablespoon of olive oil over the top and toss everything together until well mixed.
4. Serve the salad in individual bowls and top with crumbled feta and chopped basil.

Nutritional Information: Approximately 380 calories per serving, 11 g protein, 55 g carbohydrates, 14 g fat, 8 g fiber, 8 mg cholesterol, 230 mg sodium, 550 mg potassium.

Stuffed Bell Peppers with Quinoa and Black Beans
Yield: 4 servings | Prep time: 20 minutes | Cook time: 30 minutes

Ingredients:

- 4 large bell peppers, any colour
- 150g quinoa, rinsed and drained
- 300ml vegetable broth
- 1 tablespoon olive oil
- 1 small onion, diced
- 2 cloves garlic, minced
- 1 (400g) can of black beans, drained and rinsed
- 1 (400g) can of diced tomatoes, drained
- 1 teaspoon cumin
- 1/2 teaspoon chili powder
- Salt and pepper, to taste
- 50g shredded cheddar cheese
- Fresh coriander, chopped for garnish

Directions:

1. Preheat the oven to 190°C.
2. In a medium saucepan, bring the vegetable broth to a boil. Add the quinoa, reduce heat to low, cover, and simmer for 15 minutes, or until the quinoa is cooked and the liquid is absorbed. Remove from heat and set aside.
3. Cut the tops off the bell peppers and remove the seeds. Set aside.
4. In a large frying pan, heat the olive oil over medium heat. Add the onion and garlic and sauté until softened, about 5 minutes. Stir in the black beans, diced tomatoes, cumin, chili powder, salt, and pepper. Cook for another 5 minutes, stirring occasionally.
5. Combine the cooked quinoa with the bean and tomato mixture. Spoon the mixture into the bell peppers, pressing down to pack the filling. Top each pepper with a sprinkle of cheddar cheese.
6. Place the stuffed peppers in a baking dish and cover with foil. Bake for 25-30 minutes, or until the peppers are tender. Garnish with fresh coriander before serving.

Nutritional Information: Approximately 290 calories per serving, 12 g protein, 45 g carbohydrates, 8 g fat, 9 g fiber, 10 mg cholesterol, 550 mg sodium, 600 mg potassium.

Crispy Baked Falafel with Tzatziki

Yield: 4 servings | Prep time: 30 minutes | Cook time: 30 minutes

Ingredients:

For the falafel:
- 400g canned chickpeas, drained and rinsed
- 1 small onion, chopped
- 2 cloves garlic, minced
- 2 tablespoons chopped fresh parsley
- 2 tablespoons chopped fresh cilantro
- 1 teaspoon ground cumin
- 1 teaspoon ground coriander
- 1/2 teaspoon chili powder
- Salt and pepper, to taste
- 2 tablespoons whole wheat flour
- 2 tablespoons olive oil

For the tzatziki:
- 200g Greek yogurt
- 1 small cucumber, finely chopped
- 2 cloves garlic, minced
- 1 tablespoon chopped fresh dill
- 1 tablespoon lemon juice
- Salt and pepper, to taste

Directions:

1. Preheat your oven to 200°C. In a food processor, combine the chickpeas, onion, garlic, parsley, cilantro, cumin, coriander, chili powder, salt, and pepper. Process until the mixture is finely chopped but not completely smooth.
2. Transfer the mixture to a bowl and stir in the flour. Form into 12 small balls and flatten them slightly.
3. Place the falafel on a baking tray lined with parchment paper. Drizzle with the olive oil and bake for 25-30 minutes, turning once, until they are golden brown and crispy.
4. While the falafel is baking, prepare the tzatziki. In a small bowl, combine the Greek yogurt, cucumber, garlic, dill, lemon juice, salt, and pepper. Stir well to combine.
5. Serve the falafel with the tzatziki on the side.

Nutritional Information: Approximately 320 calories per serving, 14 g protein, 35 g carbohydrates, 14 g fat, 7 g fiber, 5 mg cholesterol, 420 mg sodium, 420 mg potassium.

Vegetable Pad Thai with Tofu
Yield: 4 servings | Prep time: 20 minutes | Cook time: 15 minutes

Ingredients:

- 200g rice noodles
- 1 tablespoon olive oil
- 400g firm tofu, pressed and cubed
- 1 red bell pepper, thinly sliced
- 1 yellow bell pepper, thinly sliced
- 1 small red onion, thinly sliced
- 2 carrots, julienned
- 2 cloves garlic, minced
- 100g bean sprouts
- 3 spring onions, chopped

- 50g unsalted peanuts, chopped
- 2 tablespoons chopped fresh coriander

Sauce:
- 3 tablespoons low-sodium soy sauce
- 1 tablespoon fish sauce (optional)
- 1 tablespoon tamarind paste
- 1 tablespoon brown sugar
- 1 teaspoon chili paste (adjust to taste)
- 1 lime, juiced

Directions:

1. Cook rice noodles according to package instructions, then rinse under cold water and set aside.
2. In a small bowl, mix together all the sauce ingredients until well combined. Set aside.
3. Heat olive oil in a large skillet or wok over medium heat. Add tofu and cook until browned on all sides, about 5-7 minutes. Remove tofu from the pan and set aside.
4. In the same pan, add the bell peppers, red onion, carrots, and garlic. Sauté for 3-4 minutes until vegetables are tender.
5. Add the cooked noodles, tofu, sauce, bean sprouts, and half of the spring onions to the pan. Toss everything together until well combined and heated through.
6. Serve the pad thai garnished with the remaining spring onions, chopped peanuts, and fresh coriander.

Nutritional Information: Approximately 425 calories per serving, 19 g protein, 57 g carbohydrates, 16 g fat, 5 g fiber, 0 mg cholesterol, 800 mg sodium, 600 mg potassium.

Moroccan Vegetable Tagine

Yield: 4 servings | Prep time: 15 minutes | Cook time: 40 minutes

Ingredients:

- 2 tablespoons olive oil
- 1 large onion, chopped
- 2 cloves garlic, minced
- 1 teaspoon ground cumin
- 1 teaspoon ground coriander
- 1 teaspoon ground turmeric
- 1 teaspoon paprika
- 1 teaspoon ground cinnamon
- 400g canned tomatoes, diced
- 300g butternut squash, peeled and cut into chunks
- 2 large carrots, sliced
- 1 medium courgette, sliced
- 1 medium red bell pepper, chopped
- 200g canned chickpeas, drained and rinsed
- 250ml vegetable stock
- 2 tablespoons chopped fresh coriander
- 2 tablespoons chopped fresh parsley
- Salt and pepper to taste

Directions:

1. In a large tagine or heavy-bottomed pot, heat the olive oil over medium heat. Add the onions and garlic, and sauté until the onions are translucent, about 5 minutes.
2. Add the ground cumin, ground coriander, ground turmeric, paprika, and cinnamon to the pot, stirring to coat the onions and garlic in the spices. Cook for 1-2 minutes until the spices become fragrant.
3. Add the diced tomatoes, butternut squash, carrots, courgette, and red bell pepper to the pot. Stir to combine with the onions, garlic, and spices.
4. Add the chickpeas and vegetable stock to the pot, and season with salt and pepper. Bring the mixture to a simmer, then cover and reduce heat to low. Cook for 30-35 minutes until the vegetables are tender.
5. Just before serving, stir in the chopped coriander and parsley. Serve the tagine with whole grain couscous or quinoa for a complete meal.

Nutritional Information: Approximately 300 calories per serving, 9 g protein, 54 g carbohydrates, 7 g fat, 12 g fiber, 0 mg cholesterol, 700 mg sodium, 900 mg potassium.

Spinach and Feta Spanakopita
Yield: 6 servings | Prep time: 20 minutes | Cook time: 35 minutes

Ingredients:

- 500g fresh spinach, chopped
- 1 medium onion, finely chopped
- 2 cloves garlic, minced
- 2 tablespoons olive oil
- 200g feta cheese, crumbled
- 2 large eggs, beaten
- 2 tablespoons fresh dill, chopped
- Salt and pepper to taste
- 6 sheets of phyllo pastry (each sheet about 30x40 cm)
- Olive oil spray or melted butter for brushing

Directions:

1. Preheat your oven to 180°C (160°C fan-assisted)
2. In a large pan, heat the olive oil over medium heat. Add the onion and garlic, sautéing until the onion is translucent, about 5 minutes.
3. Add the chopped spinach to the pan and cook until wilted, about 3-4 minutes. Remove from heat and let cool slightly.
4. In a mixing bowl, combine the feta cheese, beaten eggs, and dill. Add the cooled spinach mixture and season with salt and pepper. Stir until well combined.
5. Lay one sheet of phyllo pastry on a clean surface and lightly brush with olive oil spray or melted butter. Place another sheet on top and repeat until all six sheets are layered.
6. Spread the spinach and feta mixture over the phyllo pastry, leaving a small border around the edges. Roll the pastry up like a log, then carefully transfer to a baking tray lined with parchment paper. Brush the top with more olive oil spray or melted butter.
7. Bake for 30-35 minutes, or until the spanakopita is golden brown and crisp. Let cool for a few minutes before slicing and serving.

Nutritional Information: Approximately 210 calories per serving, 10 g protein, 17 g carbohydrates, 12 g fat, 3 g fiber, 70 mg cholesterol, 450 mg sodium, 500 mg potassium.

Lean Protein Classics

Baked Lemon Herb Chicken Breast
Yield: 4 servings | Prep time: 10 minutes | Cook time: 25 minutes

Ingredients:

- 4 boneless, skinless chicken breasts (about 600g)
- 2 lemons, zested and juiced
- 4 cloves garlic, minced
- 2 tablespoons olive oil
- 1 tablespoon dried oregano
- 1 tablespoon dried basil
- 1 tablespoon dried rosemary
- Salt and pepper, to taste
- Fresh parsley, for garnish (optional)

Directions:

1. Preheat your oven to 200°C.
2. In a bowl, combine the lemon zest, lemon juice, minced garlic, olive oil, oregano, basil, rosemary, salt, and pepper. Mix well.
3. Place the chicken breasts in a baking dish. Pour the lemon herb mixture over the chicken breasts, ensuring they are evenly coated.
4. Cover the baking dish with foil and bake for 20 minutes.
5. Remove the foil and bake for an additional 5 minutes, or until the chicken breasts are fully cooked and the internal temperature reaches 75°C.
6. Garnish with fresh parsley, if desired, and serve.

Nutritional Information: Approximately 260 calories per serving, 30 g protein, 5 g carbohydrates, 13 g fat, 1 g fiber, 85 mg cholesterol, 350 mg sodium, 400 mg potassium.

Pork Tenderloin with Apple Cider Glaze
Yield: 4 servings | Prep time: 10 minutes | Cook time: 30 minutes

Ingredients:

- 450g pork tenderloin
- Salt and pepper, to taste
- 2 tablespoons olive oil
- 1 small onion, finely chopped
- 2 cloves garlic, minced
- 250ml apple cider
- 2 tablespoons apple cider vinegar
- 2 tablespoons Dijon mustard
- 1 tablespoon chopped fresh thyme
- 1 tablespoon chopped fresh rosemary

Directions:

1. Preheat your oven to 190°C (375°F).
2. Season the pork tenderloin with salt and pepper on all sides.
3. In an oven-safe skillet, heat the olive oil over medium-high heat. Add the pork tenderloin and sear for about 3-4 minutes per side, until it's browned on all sides.
4. Remove the pork tenderloin from the skillet and set it aside. In the same skillet, add the chopped onion and garlic and sauté until the onion is translucent, about 3 minutes.
5. Add the apple cider, apple cider vinegar, Dijon mustard, thyme, and rosemary to the skillet. Stir to combine and bring the mixture to a simmer.
6. Return the pork tenderloin to the skillet and spoon some of the glaze over the top.
7. Transfer the skillet to the preheated oven and roast for 15-20 minutes, or until the pork is cooked through and the internal temperature reaches 63°C (145°F).
8. Remove the skillet from the oven and let the pork rest for 5 minutes before slicing and serving with the apple cider glaze.

Nutritional Information: Approximately 245 calories per serving, 27 g protein, 8 g carbohydrates, 11 g fat, 1 g fiber, 80 mg cholesterol, 220 mg sodium, 330 mg potassium.

Turkey and Zucchini Meatballs

Yield: 4 servings | Prep time: 15 minutes | Cook time: 25 minutes

Ingredients:

- 450g lean ground turkey
- 1 medium zucchini (about 200g), grated
- 1 small onion (about 70g), finely chopped
- 2 cloves garlic, minced
- 1 egg
- 50g whole wheat breadcrumbs
- 30g grated Parmesan cheese
- 1 tablespoon fresh basil, chopped
- 1 tablespoon fresh parsley, chopped
- Salt and pepper, to taste
- 2 tablespoons olive oil

Directions:

1. Preheat your oven to 200°C. In a large bowl, combine the ground turkey, grated zucchini, chopped onion, minced garlic, egg, breadcrumbs, Parmesan cheese, basil, parsley, salt, and pepper. Mix until well combined.
2. Shape the mixture into golf-ball-sized meatballs and place them on a baking tray lined with parchment paper.
3. Heat the olive oil in a large skillet over medium heat. Add the meatballs and brown them on all sides, about 2-3 minutes per side.
4. Transfer the browned meatballs to the oven and bake for 20 minutes, or until they are cooked through and the internal temperature reaches 74°C.
5. Serve the meatballs with a side of your choice.

Nutritional Information: Approximately 330 calories per serving, 31 g protein, 15 g carbohydrates, 16 g fat, 3 g fiber, 125 mg cholesterol, 320 mg sodium, 430 mg potassium.

Pan-Seared Salmon with Dill Sauce

Yield: 4 servings | Prep time: 10 minutes | Cook time: 10 minutes

Ingredients:

- 4 salmon fillets (about 150g each)
- Salt and pepper, to taste
- 2 tablespoons olive oil
- 200g Greek yogurt
- 2 tablespoons fresh dill, chopped
- 1 tablespoon lemon juice
- 1 teaspoon Dijon mustard
- 1 small clove garlic, minced
- 1 tablespoon capers, drained and chopped

Directions:

1. Season the salmon fillets with salt and pepper on both sides.
2. In a large skillet, heat the olive oil over medium-high heat. Add the salmon fillets, skin-side down, and sear for about 4 minutes. Flip the fillets and cook for an additional 3-4 minutes, or until the salmon is cooked through and flakes easily with a fork.
3. While the salmon is cooking, in a small bowl, combine the Greek yogurt, dill, lemon juice, mustard, garlic, and capers. Stir until well combined.
4. Once the salmon is cooked, remove from the skillet and place on serving plates.
5. Spoon the dill sauce over the salmon fillets and serve.

Nutritional Information: Approximately 340 calories per serving, 32 g protein, 3 g carbohydrates, 22 g fat, 0 g fiber, 85 mg cholesterol, 210 mg sodium, 520 mg potassium.

Lemon Garlic Roasted Chicken Thighs

Yield: 4 servings | Prep time: 10 minutes | Cook time: 45 minutes

Ingredients:

- 4 bone-in, skin-on chicken thighs (about 150g each)
- Salt and pepper, to taste
- 2 tablespoons olive oil
- 4 cloves garlic, minced
- Zest and juice of 1 lemon
- 1 teaspoon dried oregano
- 1 teaspoon dried thyme
- 1 teaspoon dried rosemary
- 1 tablespoon chopped fresh parsley (for garnish)

Directions:

1. Preheat your oven to 200°C (390°F).
2. Season the chicken thighs with salt and pepper on both sides.
3. In a large oven-safe skillet, heat the olive oil over medium-high heat. Add the chicken thighs, skin-side down, and sear for about 5 minutes, or until the skin is golden brown and crispy. Flip the thighs and cook for an additional 2-3 minutes.
4. In a small bowl, combine the minced garlic, lemon zest, lemon juice, oregano, thyme, and rosemary. Pour this mixture over the chicken thighs in the skillet.
5. Transfer the skillet to the preheated oven and roast for 30-35 minutes, or until the chicken is cooked through and the internal temperature reaches 75°C (165°F).
6. Remove the skillet from the oven and let the chicken rest for 5 minutes. Garnish with chopped parsley before serving.

Nutritional Information: Approximately 380 calories per serving, 30 g protein, 3 g carbohydrates, 28 g fat, 0.5 g fiber, 140 mg cholesterol, 370 mg sodium, 250 mg potassium.

Grilled Swordfish with Cilantro Lime Sauce

Yield: 4 servings | Prep time: 10 minutes | Cook time: 12 minutes

Ingredients:

- 4 swordfish steaks (about 800g)
- Salt and pepper, to taste
- 1 tablespoon olive oil
- 2 cloves garlic, minced
- 1 lime, juiced
- 1 lime, zested
- 1 bunch fresh cilantro (coriander), chopped (about 30g)
- 1/2 teaspoon chili flakes (optional)

Directions:

1. Preheat your grill to medium-high heat. Season the swordfish steaks with salt and pepper on both sides.
2. In a small bowl, whisk together the olive oil, minced garlic, lime juice, lime zest, chopped cilantro, and chili flakes (if using). Season with salt and pepper to taste.
3. Brush the swordfish steaks with some of the cilantro lime sauce and place them on the grill. Grill for about 5-6 minutes per side, or until the fish is cooked through and the internal temperature reaches 63°C.
4. Serve the grilled swordfish steaks with the remaining cilantro lime sauce drizzled on top.

Nutritional Information: Approximately 250 calories per serving, 34 g protein, 1 g carbohydrates, 12 g fat, 0.2 g fiber, 60 mg cholesterol, 160 mg sodium, 550 mg potassium.

Balsamic Glazed Grilled Chicken
Yield: 4 servings | Prep time: 10 minutes | Cook time: 20 minutes

Ingredients:

- 4 boneless, skinless chicken breasts (about 600g total)
- Salt and pepper, to taste
- 2 tablespoons olive oil
- 120ml balsamic vinegar
- 1 tablespoon honey
- 2 cloves garlic, minced
- 1 teaspoon dried rosemary
- 1 teaspoon dried thyme
- 1 tablespoon chopped fresh parsley (for garnish)

Directions:

1. Preheat your grill to medium-high heat.
2. Season the chicken breasts with salt and pepper on both sides.
3. In a small saucepan, heat the olive oil over medium heat. Add the garlic and sauté for about 1 minute until fragrant.
4. Add the balsamic vinegar, honey, rosemary, and thyme to the saucepan. Stir to combine and bring the mixture to a simmer. Reduce the heat to low and simmer for about 5-7 minutes, until the glaze has thickened slightly. Remove from heat.
5. Place the chicken breasts on the grill and cook for about 6-8 minutes per side, or until the internal temperature reaches 74°C (165°F).
6. Brush the balsamic glaze over the chicken breasts during the last few minutes of grilling.
7. Remove the chicken from the grill and let it rest for a few minutes before serving. Garnish with fresh parsley.

Nutritional Information: Approximately 220 calories per serving, 30 g protein, 10 g carbohydrates, 7 g fat, 0 g fiber, 80 mg cholesterol, 220 mg sodium, 300 mg potassium.

Rosemary Lemon Grilled Lamb Chops
Yield: 4 servings | Prep time: 10 minutes (+1 hour marinating time) | Cook time: 10 minutes

Ingredients:

- 8 lamb chops (about 800g total)
- 2 tablespoons olive oil
- 3 tablespoons freshly squeezed lemon juice
- 4 cloves garlic, minced
- 2 tablespoons fresh rosemary leaves, finely chopped
- Salt and freshly ground black pepper, to taste
- Lemon wedges, for serving

Directions:

1. In a small bowl, mix together olive oil, lemon juice, minced garlic, and chopped rosemary. Season with salt and pepper.
2. Place the lamb chops in a shallow dish or resealable plastic bag and pour the marinade over them. Ensure each chop is well coated, then cover the dish or seal the bag and refrigerate for at least 1 hour to marinate.
3. Preheat a grill or grill pan to medium-high heat. Remove the lamb chops from the marinade and let any excess marinade drip off.
4. Grill the lamb chops for about 4-5 minutes per side, depending on your desired level of doneness.
5. Remove the lamb chops from the grill and let them rest for a few minutes before serving. Serve with lemon wedges for extra zest.

Nutritional Information: Approximately 350 calories per serving, 34 g protein, 1 g carbohydrates, 23 g fat, 0 g fiber, 100 mg cholesterol, 85 mg sodium, 350 mg potassium.

Shrimp Scampi with Zucchini Noodles

Yield: 4 servings | Prep time: 15 minutes | Cook time: 10 minutes

Ingredients:

- 400g large shrimp, peeled and deveined
- Salt and pepper, to taste
- 4 medium zucchinis, spiralized into noodles (about 600g)
- 2 tablespoons olive oil
- 4 cloves garlic, minced
- 1/4 teaspoon red pepper flakes (optional)
- 120ml white wine (or chicken broth)
- 2 tablespoons freshly squeezed lemon juice
- 2 tablespoons chopped fresh parsley
- 1 tablespoon grated Parmesan cheese (optional)

Directions:

1. Season the shrimp with salt and pepper.
2. In a large skillet, heat the olive oil over medium heat. Add the garlic and red pepper flakes (if using) and sauté for about 1 minute until fragrant.
3. Add the shrimp to the skillet and cook for about 2-3 minutes on each side, until they are pink and opaque. Remove the shrimp from the skillet and set aside.
4. Add the white wine or chicken broth to the skillet and bring to a simmer. Cook for about 2 minutes, scraping up any browned bits from the bottom of the skillet.
5. Add the zucchini noodles to the skillet and cook for about 2-3 minutes, until they are just tender. Do not overcook, as they will become mushy.
6. Return the shrimp to the skillet and toss to combine with the zucchini noodles and sauce. Stir in the lemon juice and parsley.
7. Serve the shrimp scampi with zucchini noodles in individual bowls. If desired, sprinkle with grated Parmesan cheese.

Nutritional Information: Approximately 230 calories per serving, 23 g protein, 10 g carbohydrates, 10 g fat, 2 g fiber, 170 mg cholesterol, 440 mg sodium, 690 mg potassium.

Garlic Butter Baked Cod

Yield: 4 servings | Prep time: 10 minutes | Cook time: 15 minutes

Ingredients:

- 4 cod fillets (about 600g total)
- 4 tablespoons unsalted butter, melted
- 4 cloves garlic, minced
- 1 tablespoon fresh parsley, chopped
- Zest of 1 lemon
- 1 tablespoon lemon juice
- Salt and freshly ground black pepper, to taste
- Lemon wedges, for serving

Directions:

1. Preheat your oven to 200°C (180°C fan) or gas mark 6. Line a baking dish with parchment paper or lightly grease it.
2. In a small bowl, combine the melted butter, minced garlic, chopped parsley, lemon zest, and lemon juice. Season with salt and pepper.
3. Place the cod fillets in the prepared baking dish, and generously brush the garlic butter mixture over each fillet.
4. Bake in the preheated oven for about 15 minutes, or until the cod fillets are easily flaked with a fork.
5. Remove from the oven and let the cod fillets rest for a few minutes before serving. Serve with lemon wedges for extra zest.

Nutritional Information: Approximately 220 calories per serving, 32 g protein, 1 g carbohydrates, 10 g fat, 0 g fiber, 85 mg cholesterol, 150 mg sodium, 400 mg potassium.

Teriyaki Chicken Skewers

Yield: 4 servings | Prep time: 15 minutes | Cook time: 10 minutes

Ingredients:

- 400g boneless, skinless chicken breast, cut into bite-sized pieces
- 1 large red bell pepper, cut into bite-sized pieces
- 1 large green bell pepper, cut into bite-sized pieces
- 1 large red onion, cut into bite-sized pieces
- 8 wooden skewers, soaked in water for at least 30 minutes

For the Teriyaki Sauce:
- 60ml low-sodium soy sauce
- 60ml water
- 2 tablespoons erythritol (or another suitable sweetener for diabetics)
- 1 tablespoon rice vinegar
- 1 clove garlic, minced
- 1/2 teaspoon ginger, grated
- 1 teaspoon cornstarch mixed with 1 tablespoon water (optional)

Directions:

1. Preheat your grill or grill pan to medium-high heat.
2. In a small saucepan over medium heat, combine the soy sauce, water, erythritol, rice vinegar, garlic, and ginger. Bring to a simmer, stirring occasionally. If you prefer a thicker sauce, add the cornstarch and water mixture, and continue to simmer until the sauce has thickened. Remove from heat and set aside.
3. Thread the chicken, bell peppers, and onion onto the soaked skewers, alternating the ingredients.
4. Lightly brush the skewers with the teriyaki sauce.
5. Grill the skewers for about 5 minutes on each side, or until the chicken is cooked through and the vegetables are slightly charred.
6. Serve the skewers with the remaining teriyaki sauce on the side for dipping.

Nutritional Information: Approximately 180 calories per serving, 28 g protein, 8 g carbohydrates, 3 g fat, 1 g fiber, 65 mg cholesterol, 530 mg sodium, 400 mg potassium.

Lemon Herb Grilled Tilapia

Yield: 4 servings | Prep time: 10 minutes | Cook time: 10 minutes

Ingredients:

- 4 tilapia fillets (about 150g each)
- 2 tablespoons olive oil
- Zest and juice of 1 lemon
- 2 cloves garlic, minced
- 1 teaspoon dried oregano
- 1 teaspoon dried basil
- 1 teaspoon dried thyme
- Salt and pepper to taste
- Lemon wedges for serving
- Fresh herbs for garnish (optional)

Directions:

1. Preheat your grill or grill pan to medium-high heat.
2. In a small bowl, combine the olive oil, lemon zest, lemon juice, garlic, oregano, basil, thyme, salt, and pepper. Stir well to combine.
3. Brush both sides of each tilapia fillet with the lemon herb mixture.
4. Place the tilapia fillets on the grill and cook for 4-5 minutes on each side, or until the fish is opaque and flakes easily with a fork.
5. Remove the tilapia fillets from the grill and serve with lemon wedges and fresh herbs, if desired.

Nutritional Information: Approximately 205 calories per serving, 29 g protein, 2 g carbohydrates, 9 g fat, 1 g fiber, 60 mg cholesterol, 90 mg sodium, 450 mg potassium.

Stuffed Chicken Breast with Spinach and Ricotta

Yield: 4 servings | Prep time: 15 minutes | Cook time: 30 minutes

Ingredients:

- 4 boneless, skinless chicken breasts (about 150g each)
- 200g ricotta cheese
- 100g spinach, cooked and drained
- 2 cloves garlic, minced
- 1 teaspoon dried basil
- 1 teaspoon dried oregano
- 1/2 teaspoon salt
- 1/4 teaspoon black pepper
- 1 tablespoon olive oil
- Lemon wedges, for serving

Directions:

1. Preheat your oven to 200°C (180°C fan-assisted).
2. In a medium bowl, combine the ricotta, spinach, garlic, basil, oregano, salt, and pepper. Mix until well combined.
3. Cut a horizontal slit in each chicken breast to create a pocket. Be careful not to cut all the way through.
4. Stuff each chicken breast with the spinach and ricotta mixture, dividing it evenly among the four chicken breasts.
5. Heat the olive oil in an ovenproof skillet over medium-high heat. Add the stuffed chicken breasts and cook for 3 minutes on each side, or until browned.
6. Transfer the skillet to the oven and bake for 15 minutes, or until the chicken is cooked through.
7. Remove from the oven and serve with lemon wedges.

Nutritional Information: Approximately 310 calories per serving, 40 g protein, 4 g carbohydrates, 15 g fat, 1 g fiber, 120 mg cholesterol, 390 mg sodium, 490 mg potassium.

Herb-Crusted Roast Beef

Yield: 6 servings | Prep time: 15 minutes | Cook time: 60 minutes

Ingredients:

- 1.5 kg beef roast (such as topside or sirloin)
- 2 tablespoons olive oil
- 2 cloves garlic, minced
- 2 teaspoons fresh thyme, minced
- 2 teaspoons fresh rosemary, minced
- 1 teaspoon dried oregano
- 1 teaspoon dried basil
- 1 teaspoon salt
- 1/2 teaspoon black pepper
- 250 ml beef broth

Directions:

1. Preheat your oven to 220°C (200°C fan-assisted).
2. In a small bowl, mix together the olive oil, garlic, thyme, rosemary, oregano, basil, salt, and pepper. Rub the mixture all over the beef roast.
3. Place the beef roast in a roasting pan and pour the beef broth into the bottom of the pan.
4. Roast the beef in the preheated oven for 15 minutes. Reduce the oven temperature to 180°C (160°C fan-assisted) and continue roasting for about 45 minutes or until a meat thermometer inserted into the thickest part of the roast registers 58°C for medium-rare.
5. Remove the roast from the oven and let it rest for at least 10 minutes before carving.

Nutritional Information: Approximately 390 calories per serving, 45 g protein, 2 g carbohydrates, 22 g fat, 0 g fiber, 130 mg cholesterol, 460 mg sodium, 620 mg potassium.

Pan-Seared Tuna Steaks with Soy Ginger Glaze

Yield: 4 servings | Prep time: 10 minutes | Cook time: 10 minutes

Ingredients:

- 4 tuna steaks (approximately 150g each)
- 2 tablespoons olive oil
- Salt and pepper to taste

For the glaze:
- 60 ml low-sodium soy sauce
- 2 tablespoons rice vinegar
- 1 tablespoon fresh ginger, grated

- 1 tablespoon garlic, minced
- 2 teaspoons sesame oil
- 1 teaspoon honey
- 1/2 teaspoon red chili flakes (optional)
- 1 tablespoon spring onions, thinly sliced for garnish
- 1 tablespoon sesame seeds, for garnish

Directions:

1. In a small saucepan, combine the soy sauce, rice vinegar, ginger, garlic, sesame oil, honey, and red chili flakes. Bring the mixture to a simmer over medium heat and let it reduce by half, about 5 minutes. Remove from the heat and set aside.
2. Season the tuna steaks with salt and pepper on both sides. Heat olive oil in a large skillet over medium-high heat. Add the tuna steaks and sear for 2-3 minutes per side, depending on your preferred level of doneness.
3. Remove the tuna steaks from the skillet and let them rest for 2-3 minutes. Slice the steaks and arrange them on plates.
4. Drizzle the soy ginger glaze over the tuna steaks. Garnish with spring onions and sesame seeds.

Nutritional Information: Approximately 310 calories per serving, 35 g protein, 6 g carbohydrates, 16 g fat, 0 g fiber, 65 mg cholesterol, 600 mg sodium, 350 mg potassium.

Lemon Dill Grilled Shrimp

Yield: 4 servings | Prep time: 20 minutes | Cook time: 5 minutes

Ingredients:

- 500g large raw shrimp, peeled and deveined
- 2 tablespoons olive oil
- 2 garlic cloves, minced

- Zest and juice of 1 lemon
- 2 tablespoons fresh dill, chopped
- Salt and pepper, to taste

Directions:

1. In a mixing bowl, whisk together olive oil, minced garlic, lemon zest, lemon juice, dill, salt, and pepper.
2. Add the shrimp to the marinade, ensuring each shrimp is well coated. Allow the shrimp to marinate for at least 15 minutes, but not more than an hour.
3. Preheat the grill to medium-high heat. Thread the marinated shrimp onto skewers.
4. Grill the shrimp for about 2-3 minutes on each side, or until they are opaque and cooked through.
5. Once cooked, remove from grill and serve immediately.

Nutritional Information: Approximately 190 calories per serving, 25 g protein, 3 g carbohydrates, 9 g fat, 0.5 g fiber, 180 mg cholesterol, 390 mg sodium, 200 mg potassium.

Oven-Baked Trout with Lemon and Herbs
Yield: 4 servings | Prep time: 10 minutes | Cook time: 15 minutes

Ingredients:

- 4 whole trout, cleaned and gutted (about 150g each)
- 2 lemons, thinly sliced
- 4 sprigs fresh rosemary
- 4 sprigs fresh thyme
- 2 cloves garlic, minced
- 2 tablespoons olive oil
- Salt and pepper to taste

Directions:

1. Preheat your oven to 220°C. Line a baking tray with parchment paper or aluminum foil.
2. Rinse the trout under cold water and pat dry with paper towels. Season the inside and outside of each fish with salt, pepper, and minced garlic.
3. Stuff the cavity of each trout with lemon slices, rosemary, and thyme.
4. Drizzle the olive oil over the fish and place them on the prepared baking tray.
5. Bake in the preheated oven for 12-15 minutes, or until the fish flakes easily with a fork.
6. Serve the trout hot, garnished with additional lemon slices and herbs if desired.

Nutritional Information: Approximately 240 calories per serving, 26 g protein, 3 g carbohydrates, 14 g fat, 1 g fiber, 55 mg cholesterol, 70 mg sodium, 450 mg potassium.

Garlic Herb Turkey Burgers
Yield: 4 servings | Prep time: 15 minutes | Cook time: 15 minutes

Ingredients:

- 500g lean ground turkey
- 4 cloves garlic, minced
- 2 tablespoons fresh parsley, chopped
- 2 tablespoons fresh basil, chopped
- 1 teaspoon dried oregano
- 1/2 teaspoon salt
- 1/4 teaspoon black pepper
- 1 tablespoon olive oil

Directions:

1. In a large mixing bowl, combine the ground turkey, garlic, parsley, basil, oregano, salt, and pepper. Mix well until all the ingredients are well combined.
2. Divide the mixture into 4 equal portions and shape each into a patty.
3. Heat the olive oil in a large skillet over medium heat. Once the oil is hot, add the patties and cook for about 6-7 minutes per side or until the internal temperature reaches 75°C and they are cooked through.
4. Remove the burgers from the skillet and let them rest for a few minutes before serving.
5. Serve the turkey burgers on whole wheat buns with lettuce, tomato, and onion or on a bed of mixed greens for a lower-carb option.

Nutritional Information: Approximately 240 calories per serving, 26 g protein, 3 g carbohydrates, 15 g fat, 1 g fiber, 70 mg cholesterol, 390 mg sodium, 350 mg potassium.

Roasted Pork Loin with Cranberry Sauce

Yield: 6 servings | Prep time: 15 minutes | Cook time: 70 minutes

Ingredients:

- 1 kg pork loin
- Salt and pepper to taste
- 1 tablespoon olive oil
- 2 sprigs fresh rosemary, chopped
- 3 cloves garlic, minced

For the cranberry sauce:
- 200g fresh or frozen cranberries
- 60 ml orange juice
- 2 tablespoons Stevia or other sugar substitute
- 1/2 teaspoon ground cinnamon
- 1/4 teaspoon ground nutmeg
- Salt to taste

Directions:

1. Preheat your oven to 180°C. Season the pork loin with salt, pepper, rosemary, and garlic. Heat the olive oil in a large oven-safe skillet over medium-high heat. Add the pork loin and brown on all sides, approximately 3-5 minutes per side.
2. Place the skillet in the preheated oven and roast for about 60 minutes, or until the internal temperature reaches 70°C. Remove the pork loin from the oven, cover it with aluminum foil, and let it rest for 10 minutes.
3. While the pork is roasting, make the cranberry sauce. Combine the cranberries, orange juice, Stevia, cinnamon, nutmeg, and salt in a saucepan. Bring the mixture to a boil, then reduce the heat and simmer for about 10 minutes, or until the cranberries have burst and the sauce has thickened.
4. Slice the pork loin and serve with the cranberry sauce.

Nutritional Information: Approximately 280 calories per serving, 30 g protein, 15 g carbohydrates, 10 g fat, 2 g fiber, 70 mg cholesterol, 80 mg sodium, 340 mg potassium.

Savoury Snacks and Appetisers

Spinach and Artichoke Dip
Yield: 6 servings | Prep time: 10 minutes | Cook time: 25 minutes

Ingredients:

- 250g fresh spinach, chopped
- 1 can (400g) artichoke hearts, drained and chopped
- 200g low-fat cream cheese
- 100g low-fat Greek yogurt
- 50g grated Parmesan cheese
- 2 garlic cloves, minced
- Salt and pepper, to taste
- 1 tablespoon olive oil (for sautéing)
- 50g grated mozzarella cheese (for topping)

Directions:

1. Preheat your oven to 190°C.
2. In a large skillet, heat olive oil over medium heat. Add the garlic and sauté until fragrant, about 1 minute.
3. Add the chopped spinach and cook until wilted, about 2-3 minutes. Remove from heat and set aside.
4. In a large bowl, mix together the cream cheese, Greek yogurt, Parmesan cheese, salt, and pepper. Add the sautéed spinach and chopped artichokes. Mix until well combined.
5. Transfer the mixture to a baking dish and top with grated mozzarella cheese.
6. Bake for 20-25 minutes, or until the cheese is melted and the dip is bubbling.
7. Remove from oven and let cool for a few minutes before serving.

Nutritional Information: Approximately 175 calories per serving, 12 g protein, 10 g carbohydrates, 8 g fat, 3 g fiber, 25 mg cholesterol, 370 mg sodium, 225 mg potassium.

Zucchini Fritters with Garlic Aioli
Yield: 6 servings | Prep time: 20 minutes | Cook time: 15 minutes

Ingredients:

For the fritters:
- 500g zucchini, grated
- 50g almond flour
- 1 large egg, beaten
- 30g grated Parmesan cheese
- 1 clove garlic, minced
- Salt and pepper, to taste

- 2 tablespoons olive oil, for frying

For the aioli:
- 100g low-fat mayonnaise
- 1 clove garlic, minced
- 1 tablespoon lemon juice
- Salt and pepper, to taste

Directions:

1. In a large bowl, combine grated zucchini, almond flour, beaten egg, Parmesan cheese, garlic, salt, and pepper. Mix until well combined.
2. Heat olive oil in a large frying pan over medium heat.
3. Scoop spoonfuls of the zucchini mixture into the pan and flatten them with the back of the spoon. Cook for 2-3 minutes on each side, or until golden brown.
4. Transfer the fritters to a plate lined with paper towels to drain any excess oil.
5. To make the aioli, mix together mayonnaise, garlic, lemon juice, salt, and pepper in a small bowl.
6. Serve the fritters hot with the aioli on the side.

Nutritional Information: Approximately 140 calories per serving, 6 g protein, 6 g carbohydrates, 10 g fat, 2 g fiber, 35 mg cholesterol, 250 mg sodium, 300 mg potassium.

Stuffed Mini Peppers with Cream Cheese
Yield: 6 servings | Prep time: 10 minutes | Cook time: 15 minutes

Ingredients:

- 300g mini bell peppers, halved and seeds removed
- 200g low-fat cream cheese, softened
- 1 clove garlic, minced
- 30g fresh chives, chopped
- 1 tablespoon lemon juice
- Salt and pepper, to taste
- Olive oil spray

Directions:

1. Preheat your oven to 200°C (400°F).
2. In a medium-sized bowl, mix together the cream cheese, garlic, chives, lemon juice, salt, and pepper until smooth.
3. Spoon the cream cheese mixture into the halved mini bell peppers, filling each one evenly.
4. Arrange the stuffed peppers on a baking sheet lined with parchment paper.
5. Lightly spray the peppers with olive oil.
6. Bake in the preheated oven for about 15 minutes, or until the peppers are tender and the tops are lightly golden.
7. Remove from the oven and let them cool for a few minutes before serving.

Nutritional Information: Approximately 85 calories per serving, 3 g protein, 7 g carbohydrates, 5 g fat, 2 g fiber, 15 mg cholesterol, 180 mg sodium, 200 mg potassium.

Bruschetta with Tomato and Basil
Yield: 6 servings | Prep time: 10 minutes | Cook time: 5 minutes

Ingredients:

- 1 large whole-grain baguette (about 300g), sliced into 1.5cm thick rounds
- 400g ripe tomatoes, diced
- 30g fresh basil leaves, chopped
- 1 large clove garlic, minced
- 2 tablespoons extra-virgin olive oil
- 1 tablespoon balsamic vinegar
- Salt and pepper, to taste
- Olive oil spray

Directions:

1. Preheat your oven grill (broiler) to high heat.
2. Arrange the baguette slices on a baking tray, lightly spray with olive oil and grill for about 2 minutes or until they are lightly browned. Flip the slices and grill the other side.
3. In a medium bowl, combine the diced tomatoes, chopped basil, minced garlic, extra-virgin olive oil, balsamic vinegar, salt, and pepper. Stir well to mix.
4. Spoon the tomato and basil mixture evenly over the grilled baguette slices.
5. Serve immediately as an appetizer or snack.

Nutritional Information: Approximately 180 calories per serving, 6 g protein, 30 g carbohydrates, 5 g fat, 4 g fiber, 0 mg cholesterol, 240 mg sodium, 350 mg potassium.

Baked Mozzarella Sticks

Yield: 6 servings | Prep time: 10 minutes | Cook time: 10 minutes

Ingredients:

- 12 part-skim mozzarella cheese sticks, halved (about 300g)
- 60g whole wheat breadcrumbs
- 1 teaspoon Italian seasoning
- 1/2 teaspoon garlic powder
- 1/4 teaspoon ground black pepper
- 2 large egg whites
- Olive oil spray

Directions:

1. Preheat your oven to 220°C (425°F) and line a baking tray with parchment paper or a silicone baking mat.
2. In a shallow dish, combine the breadcrumbs, Italian seasoning, garlic powder, and black pepper.
3. In another shallow dish, lightly beat the egg whites.
4. Dip each mozzarella stick half into the egg whites, letting any excess drip off, and then roll it in the breadcrumb mixture, pressing gently to adhere. Place the coated mozzarella sticks on the prepared baking tray.
5. Lightly spray the coated mozzarella sticks with olive oil spray.
6. Bake for 8-10 minutes or until the sticks are golden brown and the cheese starts to melt.
7. Serve immediately with marinara sauce or another dipping sauce of your choice.

Nutritional Information: Approximately 150 calories per serving, 9 g protein, 9 g carbohydrates, 8 g fat, 1 g fiber, 15 mg cholesterol, 270 mg sodium, 40 mg potassium.

Vegetable Spring Rolls with Soy Dipping Sauce

Yield: 6 servings | Prep time: 30 minutes | Cook time: 10 minutes

Ingredients:

For the Spring Rolls:
- 12 rice paper wrappers (about 220g)
- 150g shredded carrots
- 150g thinly sliced cucumber
- 150g thinly sliced red bell pepper
- 100g shredded red cabbage
- 75g fresh mint leaves
- 75g fresh basil leaves
- 75g fresh cilantro leaves
- Water, for softening rice paper

For the Soy Dipping Sauce:
- 60 ml soy sauce (low sodium)
- 30 ml rice vinegar
- 15 ml sesame oil
- 1 teaspoon minced garlic
- 1 teaspoon grated ginger
- 1 tablespoon chopped green onion
- 1/2 teaspoon chili flakes (optional)
- 1 tablespoon sesame seeds (optional)

Directions:

1. Prepare the soy dipping sauce by combining all sauce ingredients in a small bowl. Whisk well and set aside.
2. Fill a shallow dish with water. One at a time, dip the rice paper wrappers into the water for about 10-15 seconds until softened. Lay the rice paper on a clean, damp kitchen towel.
3. Place a small amount of each vegetable and a few leaves of mint, basil, and cilantro on the lower third of the rice paper. Fold the bottom of the rice paper over the filling, then fold in the sides and roll it up tightly.
4. Repeat with the remaining rice paper wrappers and filling.
5. Serve the spring rolls immediately with the soy dipping sauce.

Nutritional Information: Approximately 150 calories per serving, 3 g protein, 31 g carbohydrates, 2 g fat, 2 g fiber, 0 mg cholesterol, 450 mg sodium, 150 mg potassium.

Greek Spanakopita Triangles

Yield: 6 servings | Prep time: 30 minutes | Cook time: 20 minutes

Ingredients:

- 300g fresh spinach, chopped
- 200g feta cheese, crumbled
- 100g onion, finely chopped
- 2 cloves garlic, minced
- 2 large eggs, beaten
- 1 tablespoon olive oil
- 1 teaspoon dried dill
- 1/2 teaspoon ground nutmeg
- 12 sheets phyllo dough, thawed
- 60 ml olive oil, for brushing
- Salt and pepper to taste

Directions:

1. Preheat the oven to 180°C (350°F). Line a baking sheet with parchment paper.
2. In a large skillet, heat the olive oil over medium heat. Add the onion and garlic, and sauté until translucent, about 3-4 minutes. Add the chopped spinach and cook until wilted, about 2-3 minutes. Remove from heat and let it cool.
3. In a mixing bowl, combine the spinach mixture, crumbled feta, beaten eggs, dill, nutmeg, salt, and pepper. Mix well.
4. Lay one sheet of phyllo dough on a clean surface. Brush it lightly with olive oil. Place another sheet on top and brush with olive oil again. Cut the double layer of phyllo into 4 equal strips.
5. Place a spoonful of the spinach mixture at the bottom of each strip. Fold the bottom of the strip over the filling to form a triangle. Continue folding up the strip in a triangle shape, like folding a flag, until you reach the end of the strip. Repeat with the remaining phyllo and filling.
6. Place the triangles on the prepared baking sheet and brush the tops with olive oil. Bake for 15-20 minutes, or until golden brown and crispy.
7. Serve hot.

Nutritional Information: Approximately 250 calories per serving, 10 g protein, 18 g carbohydrates, 16 g fat, 2 g fiber, 80 mg cholesterol, 350 mg sodium, 250 mg potassium.

Prosciutto Wrapped Asparagus

Yield: 4 servings | Prep time: 10 minutes | Cook time: 15 minutes

Ingredients:

- 16 asparagus spears, trimmed
- 8 thin slices of prosciutto, halved
- 1 tablespoon olive oil
- 1 tablespoon balsamic vinegar
- Salt and pepper to taste
- 2 tablespoons grated Parmesan cheese (optional)

Directions:

1. Preheat your oven to 200°C (400°F).
2. Wrap each asparagus spear with a half slice of prosciutto, starting at the bottom and winding your way up to the top.
3. Place the wrapped asparagus on a baking sheet, and drizzle with olive oil and balsamic vinegar. Season with a little salt and pepper.
4. Bake for 10-15 minutes, or until the asparagus is tender and the prosciutto is crisp.
5. If desired, sprinkle with grated Parmesan cheese before serving.

Nutritional Information: Approximately 100 calories per serving, 7 g protein, 4 g carbohydrates, 7 g fat, 2 g fiber, 10 mg cholesterol, 340 mg sodium, 220 mg potassium.

Spinach and Ricotta Stuffed Mushrooms

Yield: 4 servings | Prep time: 15 minutes | Cook time: 25 minutes

Ingredients:

- 16 large mushrooms, stems removed
- 200g fresh spinach, chopped
- 200g ricotta cheese
- 100g grated Parmesan cheese
- 2 cloves garlic, minced
- 1 tablespoon olive oil
- Salt and pepper to taste
- 2 tablespoons chopped fresh basil
- 1 tablespoon lemon zest

Directions:

1. Preheat the oven to 180°C (350°F). Grease a baking dish with olive oil.
2. In a large skillet, heat the olive oil over medium heat. Add the garlic and sauté for 1-2 minutes, until fragrant. Add the spinach and cook until wilted, about 2-3 minutes. Remove from heat and allow it to cool.
3. In a mixing bowl, combine the cooled spinach, ricotta, half of the grated Parmesan, basil, lemon zest, salt, and pepper. Mix until well combined.
4. Spoon the spinach and ricotta mixture into the mushroom caps, pressing down gently to pack the filling. Sprinkle the remaining Parmesan on top.
5. Place the stuffed mushrooms in the prepared baking dish and bake for 20-25 minutes, or until the mushrooms are tender and the cheese is melted and slightly golden.
6. Serve hot.

Nutritional Information: Approximately 210 calories per serving, 14 g protein, 6 g carbohydrates, 14 g fat, 2 g fiber, 30 mg cholesterol, 350 mg sodium, 450 mg potassium.

Spicy Deviled Eggs

Yield: 4 servings | Prep time: 20 minutes | Cook time: 10 minutes

Ingredients:

- 8 large eggs
- 4 tablespoons mayonnaise
- 1 teaspoon Dijon mustard
- 1 teaspoon white wine vinegar
- 1/2 teaspoon smoked paprika
- 1/4 teaspoon cayenne pepper
- Salt and pepper, to taste
- 1 small red chili pepper, finely chopped (for garnish)
- Fresh parsley, chopped (for garnish)

Directions:

1. Place the eggs in a medium saucepan and cover them with water. Bring to a boil over high heat. Once boiling, reduce the heat to low, cover the pan, and simmer for 10 minutes.
2. After the eggs have cooked, transfer them to a bowl of cold water and let them cool completely. Peel the eggs and cut them in half lengthwise.
3. Remove the yolks from the eggs and place them in a medium bowl. Mash the yolks with a fork until smooth.
4. Add the mayonnaise, mustard, vinegar, paprika, cayenne pepper, salt, and pepper to the bowl with the yolks. Mix well until the filling is smooth and creamy.
5. Spoon or pipe the filling back into the egg whites. Garnish with the chopped chili pepper and parsley.
6. Serve immediately or refrigerate until ready to serve.

Nutritional Information: Approximately 180 calories per serving, 10 g protein, 2 g carbohydrates, 15 g fat, 0 g fiber, 220 mg cholesterol, 250 mg sodium, 90 mg potassium.

Smoked Salmon and Cream Cheese Pinwheels

Yield: 4 servings | Prep time: 15 minutes | Cook time: 0 minutes

Ingredients:

- 4 whole grain tortillas (approximately 20 cm diameter)
- 200 g cream cheese, softened
- 2 tablespoons fresh dill, finely chopped
- Zest of 1 lemon
- 200 g smoked salmon
- 1 small red onion, thinly sliced
- 2 tablespoons capers, drained

Directions:

1. In a small bowl, combine the cream cheese, dill, and lemon zest. Stir until well mixed.
2. Lay out the tortillas on a clean surface. Spread the cream cheese mixture evenly on each tortilla.
3. Layer the smoked salmon, red onion, and capers on top of the cream cheese.
4. Roll each tortilla tightly, wrap in cling film, and refrigerate for at least 1 hour.
5. After chilling, remove the cling film and slice each tortilla roll into 2.5 cm (1-inch) thick pinwheels. Serve immediately or refrigerate until ready to serve.

Nutritional Information: Approximately 220 calories per serving, 12 g protein, 18 g carbohydrates, 12 g fat, 2 g fiber, 30 mg cholesterol, 680 mg sodium, 180 mg potassium.

Mini Cauliflower Pizzas

Yield: 6 servings | Prep time: 15 minutes | Cook time: 25 minutes

Ingredients:

- 1 medium cauliflower (about 600 g), cut into florets
- 1 large egg, beaten
- 80 g grated mozzarella cheese
- 2 tablespoons grated Parmesan cheese
- 1/2 teaspoon dried oregano
- 1/2 teaspoon garlic powder
- Salt and pepper, to taste
- 120 g low-sodium marinara sauce
- 100 g cherry tomatoes, sliced
- 1/2 small red onion, thinly sliced
- 1/4 cup (8 g) fresh basil leaves, chopped

Directions:

1. Preheat your oven to 220°C (425°F) and line two baking sheets with parchment paper.
2. Process the cauliflower florets in a food processor until they resemble fine crumbs. Transfer the cauliflower to a microwave-safe bowl, cover with plastic wrap, and microwave for 5-6 minutes or until softened.
3. Allow the cauliflower to cool for a few minutes, then transfer to a clean kitchen towel and wring out as much moisture as possible.
4. In a large bowl, combine the drained cauliflower, egg, 40 g of mozzarella cheese, Parmesan, oregano, garlic powder, salt, and pepper. Mix well.
5. Divide the cauliflower mixture into 12 equal portions and shape each into a small, flat round on the prepared baking sheets.
6. Bake the cauliflower crusts for 10-12 minutes or until they start to turn golden.
7. Remove the crusts from the oven, and spread a tablespoon of marinara sauce over each. Top with the remaining mozzarella cheese, sliced tomatoes, and red onion.
8. Return the pizzas to the oven and bake for an additional 7-10 minutes or until the cheese is melted and bubbly.
9. Sprinkle fresh basil over the pizzas before serving.

Nutritional Information: Approximately 75 calories per serving, 6 g protein, 8 g carbohydrates, 2 g fat, 3 g fiber, 30 mg cholesterol, 150 mg sodium, 320 mg potassium.

Caprese Skewers with Balsamic Drizzle

Yield: 4 servings | Prep time: 10 minutes | Cook time: 10 minutes

Ingredients:

- 24 cherry tomatoes
- 24 mini mozzarella balls (about 200 g)
- 24 fresh basil leaves
- 1/2 cup (120 ml) balsamic vinegar
- 1 tablespoon (15 ml) olive oil
- 1/4 teaspoon black pepper
- Salt, to taste
- 8 skewers

Directions:

1. In a small saucepan, bring the balsamic vinegar to a boil over medium-high heat. Reduce the heat to low and simmer for about 10 minutes, or until the vinegar is reduced by half and has a syrupy consistency. Allow the balsamic reduction to cool to room temperature.
2. While the balsamic reduction is cooling, assemble the skewers. Thread one cherry tomato, one basil leaf, and one mini mozzarella ball onto each skewer. Repeat the process until all skewers are assembled.
3. Drizzle the skewers with olive oil and season with salt and pepper
4. Arrange the skewers on a serving platter and drizzle with the balsamic reduction.
5. Serve immediately.

Nutritional Information: Approximately 125 calories per serving, 7 g protein, 5 g carbohydrates, 8 g fat, 1 g fiber, 20 mg cholesterol, 210 mg sodium, 135 mg potassium.

Crispy Baked Zucchini Chips

Yield: 4 servings | Prep time: 15 minutes | Cook time: 30 minutes

Ingredients:

- 2 medium zucchinis (about 500 g)
- 2 tablespoons (30 ml) olive oil
- 60 g grated Parmesan cheese
- 30 g almond flour
- 1/2 teaspoon garlic powder
- 1/2 teaspoon onion powder
- 1/4 teaspoon paprika
- Salt and pepper to taste

Directions:

1. Preheat your oven to 220°C (425°F) and line a baking sheet with parchment paper.
2. Slice the zucchinis into thin, even rounds (about 3 mm thick).
3. In a mixing bowl, toss the zucchini slices with olive oil to coat them evenly.
4. In another bowl, combine the grated Parmesan cheese, almond flour, garlic powder, onion powder, paprika, salt, and pepper. Mix well.
5. Dip each zucchini slice into the Parmesan mixture, ensuring both sides are coated, and place them in a single layer on the prepared baking sheet.
6. Bake for 25-30 minutes, or until the zucchini chips are golden brown and crispy. Rotate the baking sheet halfway through the cooking time for even baking.
7. Remove from the oven and allow to cool slightly before serving.

Nutritional Information: Approximately 150 calories per serving, 6 g protein, 5 g carbohydrates, 12 g fat, 2 g fiber, 10 mg cholesterol, 180 mg sodium, 290 mg potassium.

Lemon Herb Hummus

Yield: 6 servings | Prep time: 10 minutes | Cook time: 0 minutes

Ingredients:

- 400 g canned chickpeas, drained and rinsed
- 3 tablespoons (45 ml) fresh lemon juice
- 2 tablespoons (30 ml) olive oil
- 2 tablespoons (30 ml) tahini
- 1 clove garlic, minced
- 1/2 teaspoon dried basil
- 1/2 teaspoon dried oregano
- 1/2 teaspoon dried thyme
- Salt and pepper, to taste
- 2-3 tablespoons (30-45 ml) water, as needed
- Fresh herbs for garnish (optional)

Directions:

1. In a food processor, combine the chickpeas, lemon juice, olive oil, tahini, garlic, basil, oregano, thyme, salt, and pepper. Process until smooth, scraping down the sides as needed.
2. If the hummus is too thick, add water 1 tablespoon at a time, and process until the desired consistency is reached.
3. Taste and adjust the seasoning as necessary.
4. Transfer the hummus to a serving bowl, drizzle with a little extra olive oil, and garnish with fresh herbs if desired.
5. Serve with fresh vegetables, whole wheat pita bread, or crackers for a healthy and delicious snack or appetizer.

Nutritional Information: Approximately 140 calories per serving, 5 g protein, 15 g carbohydrates, 8 g fat, 4 g fiber, 0 mg cholesterol, 190 mg sodium, 140 mg potassium.

Baked Avocado Fries

Yield: 4 servings | Prep time: 15 minutes | Cook time: 15 minutes

Ingredients:

- 2 ripe avocados, pitted and peeled
- 1/2 cup (60 g) almond flour
- 1/2 teaspoon paprika
- 1/2 teaspoon garlic powder
- Salt and pepper, to taste
- 2 large eggs, lightly beaten
- 1 cup (60 g) whole-grain breadcrumbs

Directions:

1. Preheat the oven to 220°C (425°F) and line a baking sheet with parchment paper.
2. Slice each avocado into 8 wedges, and set aside.
3. In a shallow bowl, mix together the almond flour, paprika, garlic powder, salt, and pepper.
4. In another shallow bowl, beat the eggs.
5. In a third shallow bowl, add the whole-grain breadcrumbs.
6. Dredge each avocado wedge in the almond flour mixture, then dip it into the eggs, and finally coat it with the breadcrumbs. Place the coated avocado wedges onto the prepared baking sheet.
7. Bake for 12-15 minutes or until the avocado fries are crispy and golden brown.
8. Serve immediately with your choice of dipping sauce.

Nutritional Information: Approximately 250 calories per serving, 8 g protein, 19 g carbohydrates, 18 g fat, 9 g fiber, 95 mg cholesterol, 180 mg sodium, 520 mg potassium.

Crab Stuffed Mushrooms

Yield: 6 servings | Prep time: 15 minutes | Cook time: 25 minutes

Ingredients:

- 24 medium button mushrooms (about 400 g), stems removed and finely chopped
- 200 g crab meat, drained and flaked
- 60 g cream cheese, softened
- 30 g grated Parmesan cheese
- 2 green onions, finely chopped
- 1 garlic clove, minced
- 1/2 teaspoon dried thyme
- 1/2 teaspoon paprika
- Salt and pepper, to taste
- 2 tablespoons olive oil
- 2 tablespoons chopped fresh parsley for garnish

Directions:

1. Preheat your oven to 180°C (350°F) and grease a large baking dish with olive oil.
2. In a medium bowl, combine the crab meat, cream cheese, Parmesan cheese, chopped mushroom stems, green onions, garlic, thyme, paprika, salt, and pepper. Mix well.
3. Fill each mushroom cap with a generous spoonful of the crab mixture and arrange them in the prepared baking dish.
4. Drizzle the stuffed mushrooms with olive oil and bake for 20-25 minutes or until the mushrooms are tender and the filling is golden brown.
5. Remove the mushrooms from the oven and sprinkle with chopped parsley before serving.

Nutritional Information: Approximately 115 calories per serving, 9 g protein, 5 g carbohydrates, 7 g fat, 1 g fiber, 35 mg cholesterol, 250 mg sodium, 300 mg potassium.

Greek Tzatziki and Veggie Platter

Yield: 4 servings | Prep time: 20 minutes | Cook time: 0 minutes

Ingredients:

For the Tzatziki:
- 250 g Greek yogurt (low-fat)
- 1/2 large cucumber, deseeded and finely grated (about 100 g)
- 2 cloves garlic, minced
- 2 tablespoons fresh dill, finely chopped
- 1 tablespoon lemon juice
- 1 tablespoon olive oil
- Salt and pepper, to taste
- For the Veggie Platter:
- 200 g cherry tomatoes, halved
- 200 g cucumber, sliced
- 200 g bell peppers, sliced
- 200 g baby carrots
- 100 g pitted Kalamata olives

Directions:

1. In a medium bowl, mix together Greek yogurt, grated cucumber, minced garlic, chopped dill, lemon juice, and olive oil. Season with salt and pepper to taste.
2. Cover the bowl with plastic wrap and refrigerate for at least 1 hour to allow the flavors to meld.
3. While the tzatziki is chilling, prepare the veggie platter by arranging the halved cherry tomatoes, sliced cucumber, sliced bell peppers, baby carrots, and Kalamata olives on a large serving platter.
4. Serve the tzatziki alongside the veggie platter, using the veggies as dippers.
5. Garnish with extra dill, if desired, and enjoy as a refreshing and healthy appetizer.

Nutritional Information: Approximately 150 calories per serving, 6 g protein, 16 g carbohydrates, 8 g fat, 4 g fiber, 5 mg cholesterol, 350 mg sodium, 500 mg potassium.

Baked Sweet Potato Wedges with Chipotle Aioli

Yield: 4 servings | Prep time: 15 minutes | Cook time: 30 minutes

Ingredients:

For the Sweet Potato Wedges:
- 2 large sweet potatoes, cut into wedges (approximately 800 g)
- 2 tablespoons olive oil
- 1 teaspoon smoked paprika
- 1 teaspoon garlic powder
- 1/2 teaspoon salt
- 1/2 teaspoon black pepper

For the Chipotle Aioli:
- 100 g mayonnaise (low-fat)
- 1 tablespoon chipotle pepper in adobo sauce, finely chopped
- 1 clove garlic, minced
- 1 tablespoon lemon juice
- Salt and pepper, to taste

Directions:

1. Preheat your oven to 200°C (400°F) and line a baking sheet with parchment paper.
2. In a large bowl, toss sweet potato wedges with olive oil, smoked paprika, garlic powder, salt, and pepper. Spread the seasoned wedges in a single layer on the prepared baking sheet.
3. Bake in the preheated oven for 30 minutes, flipping the wedges halfway through, until they are golden brown and crispy on the outside, and tender on the inside.
4. While the wedges are baking, prepare the chipotle aioli by mixing together mayonnaise, chopped chipotle pepper, minced garlic, and lemon juice in a small bowl. Season with salt and pepper to taste.
5. Serve the baked sweet potato wedges warm, accompanied by the chipotle aioli for dipping.

Nutritional Information: Approximately 220 calories per serving, 3 g protein, 25 g carbohydrates, 12 g fat, 4 g fiber, 5 mg cholesterol, 350 mg sodium, 450 mg potassium.

Hearty Main Courses

Lemon Herb Grilled Shrimp

Yield: 4 servings | Prep time: 15 minutes | Cook time: 6 minutes

Ingredients:

- 400 g large shrimp, peeled and deveined
- 2 tablespoons olive oil
- 2 cloves garlic, minced
- Zest of 1 lemon
- 2 tablespoons fresh lemon juice
- 1 tablespoon fresh parsley, chopped
- 1 tablespoon fresh basil, chopped
- 1 tablespoon fresh thyme, chopped
- Salt and freshly ground black pepper, to taste
- Lemon wedges, for serving

Directions:

1. In a large bowl, whisk together the olive oil, garlic, lemon zest, lemon juice, parsley, basil, thyme, salt, and pepper.
2. Add the shrimp to the bowl and toss to coat with the marinade. Let the shrimp marinate for about 10 minutes.
3. Preheat the grill or a grill pan to medium-high heat. Thread the shrimp onto skewers.
4. Grill the shrimp for about 2-3 minutes per side, or until they are pink and opaque.
5. Serve the grilled shrimp hot with lemon wedges on the side.

Nutritional Information: Approximately 180 calories per serving, 24 g protein, 2 g carbohydrates, 8 g fat, 0 g fiber, 180 mg cholesterol, 180 mg sodium, 220 mg potassium.

Grilled Pork Chops with Peach Salsa

Yield: 4 servings | Prep time: 15 minutes | Cook time: 15 minutes

Ingredients:

- 4 boneless pork chops, about 2.5 cm thick (approx. 600 g total)
- 1 tablespoon olive oil
- Salt and freshly ground black pepper, to taste
- 2 ripe peaches, pitted and diced (approx. 300 g)
- 1 small red onion, finely chopped (approx. 100 g)
- 1 small red chilli, seeded and finely chopped
- 2 tablespoons chopped fresh coriander (cilantro)
- 1 lime, juice and zest
- 1 tablespoon balsamic vinegar
- 1 tablespoon extra-virgin olive oil

Directions:

1. Preheat your grill or barbecue to medium-high heat. Rub the pork chops with olive oil and season them with salt and pepper. Grill the pork chops for about 6-7 minutes per side, or until they reach an internal temperature of 62°C (145°F). Remove from the grill and let them rest for a few minutes.
2. In a medium bowl, combine the diced peaches, chopped red onion, chopped chilli, chopped coriander, lime juice, lime zest, balsamic vinegar, and extra-virgin olive oil. Stir to combine and season with salt and pepper to taste.
3. Serve the grilled pork chops topped with the peach salsa.

Nutritional Information: Approximately 300 calories per serving, 30 g protein, 15 g carbohydrates, 15 g fat, 3 g fiber, 75 mg cholesterol, 500 mg sodium, 600 mg potassium.

Lemon Butter Baked Salmon

Yield: 4 servings | Prep time: 10 minutes | Cook time: 15 minutes

Ingredients:

- 4 salmon fillets (approx. 150 g each)
- 4 tablespoons unsalted butter, melted
- 2 tablespoons fresh lemon juice
- 2 cloves garlic, minced
- Zest of 1 lemon
- 1 teaspoon dried thyme
- 1 teaspoon dried parsley
- Salt and freshly ground black pepper, to taste
- 1 lemon, sliced
- Fresh parsley, chopped for garnish

Directions:

1. Preheat your oven to 200°C (180°C fan assisted). Line a baking tray with parchment paper or aluminum foil.
2. In a small bowl, combine the melted butter, lemon juice, minced garlic, lemon zest, dried thyme, dried parsley, salt, and black pepper.
3. Place the salmon fillets on the prepared baking tray, skin-side down. Brush the butter mixture over the salmon fillets, making sure to coat them evenly.
4. Arrange the lemon slices on top of the salmon fillets.
5. Bake the salmon in the preheated oven for about 12-15 minutes, or until the salmon flakes easily with a fork. Garnish with chopped fresh parsley and serve immediately.

Nutritional Information: Approximately 280 calories per serving, 24 g protein, 1 g carbohydrates, 20 g fat, 0 g fiber, 70 mg cholesterol, 200 mg sodium, 300 mg potassium.

Teriyaki Glazed Salmon

Yield: 4 servings | Prep time: 10 minutes | Cook time: 20 minutes

Ingredients:

- 4 salmon fillets (about 600 g total)
- 2 tablespoons olive oil
- Salt and black pepper to taste
- For the teriyaki glaze:
- 60 ml low-sodium soy sauce
- 2 tablespoons sugar substitute (such as stevia or erythritol)
- 1 clove garlic, minced
- 1 teaspoon fresh ginger, grated
- 1 tablespoon rice vinegar
- 1 teaspoon sesame oil
- 1 tablespoon cornstarch
- 2 tablespoons cold water

Directions:

1. Preheat the oven to 190°C (375°F).
2. In a small saucepan, combine soy sauce, sugar substitute, minced garlic, grated ginger, rice vinegar, and sesame oil. Bring the mixture to a simmer over medium heat.
3. In a small bowl, whisk together cornstarch and cold water until smooth. Add this mixture to the saucepan and whisk constantly until the sauce thickens, about 2 minutes. Remove the pan from the heat.
4. Heat the olive oil in an ovenproof skillet over medium-high heat. Season the salmon fillets with salt and pepper, then place them skin-side down in the skillet. Cook for 3-4 minutes until the skin is crispy.
5. Flip the salmon fillets and pour the teriyaki glaze over them. Transfer the skillet to the oven and bake for 7-10 minutes until the salmon is cooked through and flakes easily with a fork.
6. Serve the teriyaki glazed salmon with your choice of vegetables or whole grain rice.

Nutritional Information: Approximately 300 calories per serving, 34 g protein, 9 g carbohydrates, 14 g fat, 0.5 g fiber, 85 mg cholesterol, 600 mg sodium, 540 mg potassium.

Baked Spaghetti Squash Carbonara

Yield: 4 servings | Prep time: 15 minutes | Cook time: 50 minutes

Ingredients:

- 1 medium spaghetti squash (about 1.5 kg)
- 2 tablespoons olive oil
- 4 rashers of lean bacon, diced (approximately 100 g)
- 2 cloves garlic, minced
- 200 g mushrooms, sliced
- 2 large eggs
- 50 g grated Parmesan cheese
- 50 g grated pecorino cheese
- Salt and freshly ground black pepper, to taste
- 2 tablespoons chopped fresh parsley

Directions:

1. Preheat your oven to 190°C (375°F). Cut the spaghetti squash in half lengthwise and scoop out the seeds. Drizzle the inside of the squash with olive oil and season with salt and pepper. Place the squash halves cut-side down on a baking sheet lined with parchment paper. Bake for 40 minutes or until the squash is tender and can be easily shredded with a fork.
2. In a large frying pan, cook the diced bacon over medium heat until crispy. Remove the bacon from the pan and set aside, leaving the rendered fat in the pan. Add the garlic and mushrooms to the pan and sauté until the mushrooms are tender.
3. In a small bowl, whisk together the eggs, Parmesan cheese, and pecorino cheese. Season with salt and pepper.
4. Once the spaghetti squash is baked, let it cool slightly before using a fork to scrape out the strands into a large mixing bowl. Add the cooked bacon, sautéed mushrooms, and garlic to the bowl. Pour the egg and cheese mixture over the spaghetti squash and toss until well combined.
5. Transfer the mixture back into the hollowed-out spaghetti squash shells. Bake for an additional 10 minutes at 190°C (375°F) or until the top is golden and the carbonara sauce has thickened.
6. Garnish with chopped fresh parsley before serving.

Nutritional Information: Approximately 350 calories per serving, 18 g protein, 28 g carbohydrates, 20 g fat, 5 g fiber, 105 mg cholesterol, 540 mg sodium, 500 mg potassium.

Baked Cod with Tomato and Basil

Yield: 4 servings | Prep time: 10 minutes | Cook time: 20 minutes

Ingredients:

- 4 cod fillets (about 150g each)
- 2 tablespoons olive oil
- Salt and pepper, to taste
- 4 medium tomatoes (about 400g), sliced
- 1 small red onion (about 100g), thinly sliced
- 2 cloves garlic, minced
- 10 fresh basil leaves, chopped
- 2 tablespoons balsamic vinegar

Directions:

1. Preheat your oven to 200°C (180°C fan, gas mark 6).
2. In a baking dish, drizzle 1 tablespoon of olive oil. Place the cod fillets in the dish and season with salt and pepper.
3. In a medium bowl, combine the sliced tomatoes, red onion, garlic, chopped basil, and balsamic vinegar. Mix well.
4. Spoon the tomato-basil mixture over the cod fillets, ensuring that each fillet is covered.
5. Drizzle the remaining 1 tablespoon of olive oil over the top of the tomato-basil mixture.
6. Bake in the preheated oven for about 20 minutes, or until the cod fillets are opaque and flake easily with a fork. Serve the baked cod hot with the tomato-basil mixture on top.

Nutritional Information: Approximately 230 calories per serving, 27 g protein, 8 g carbohydrates, 10 g fat, 2 g fiber, 60 mg cholesterol, 140 mg sodium, 620 mg potassium.

Slow Cooker Pulled Pork with Coleslaw

Yield: 6 servings | Prep time: 20 minutes | Cook time: 480 minutes

Ingredients:

For the pulled pork:

- 1.5 kg pork shoulder
- 1 teaspoon salt
- 1 teaspoon black pepper
- 1 teaspoon smoked paprika
- 1 teaspoon cumin
- 240 ml water
- 2 tablespoons apple cider vinegar
- 2 tablespoons Worcestershire sauce
- 1 onion, sliced

For the coleslaw:

- 200 g cabbage, shredded
- 1 large carrot, grated
- 60 ml Greek yogurt
- 1 tablespoon Dijon mustard
- 2 tablespoons apple cider vinegar
- 1 teaspoon honey
- Salt and freshly ground black pepper, to taste

Directions:

1. In a small bowl, combine salt, black pepper, smoked paprika, and cumin. Rub the spice mix all over the pork shoulder.
2. In the slow cooker, add water, apple cider vinegar, Worcestershire sauce, and sliced onion. Place the pork shoulder on top of the onions.
3. Cover and cook on low for 8 hours or until the pork is tender and easily shreds.
4. Once cooked, remove the pork from the slow cooker and shred it using two forks.
5. For the coleslaw, in a large bowl, combine the shredded cabbage and grated carrot. In a small bowl, whisk together Greek yogurt, Dijon mustard, apple cider vinegar, honey, salt, and black pepper. Pour the dressing over the cabbage and carrot mixture and toss to combine.
6. Serve the pulled pork on a plate or in a lettuce wrap, topped with coleslaw.

Nutritional Information: Approximately 350 calories per serving, 38 g protein, 8 g carbohydrates, 18 g fat, 2 g fiber, 120 mg cholesterol, 590 mg sodium, 480 mg potassium.

Roast Beef with Garlic Herb Crust

Yield: 6 servings | Prep time: 15 minutes | Cook time: 60 minutes

Ingredients:

- 1.5 kg beef sirloin or ribeye roast
- 6 cloves garlic, minced
- 2 tablespoons fresh rosemary, finely chopped
- 2 tablespoons fresh thyme, finely chopped
- 1 tablespoon Dijon mustard
- 2 tablespoons olive oil
- Salt and black pepper to taste

Directions:

1. Preheat the oven to 220°C (425°F).
2. In a small bowl, mix together the minced garlic, chopped rosemary, chopped thyme, Dijon mustard, olive oil, salt, and pepper.
3. Rub the garlic herb mixture all over the beef roast, ensuring it's evenly coated.
4. Place the beef roast on a rack in a roasting pan, fat-side up. Roast in the preheated oven for 15 minutes.
5. Reduce the oven temperature to 180°C (350°F) and continue roasting for 45 minutes or until a meat thermometer inserted into the thickest part of the roast reads 60°C (140°F) for medium-rare.
6. Remove the roast from the oven and let it rest for 10-15 minutes before slicing. This allows the juices to redistribute throughout the meat, ensuring a moist and flavorful roast.

Nutritional Information: Approximately 400 calories per serving, 50 g protein, 1 g carbohydrates, 21 g fat, 0.2 g fiber, 145 mg cholesterol, 350 mg sodium, 650 mg potassium.

Lemon and Herb Roasted Chicken

Yield: 4 servings | Prep time: 15 minutes | Cook time: 60 minutes

Ingredients:

- 1 whole chicken, about 1.5kg
- 2 lemons, one sliced and one juiced
- 3 cloves garlic, minced
- 2 tablespoons olive oil
- 1 teaspoon salt

- 1/2 teaspoon black pepper
- 1 tablespoon dried rosemary
- 1 tablespoon dried thyme
- 1 tablespoon dried oregano
- 2 tablespoons fresh parsley, chopped

Directions:

1. Preheat your oven to 190°C (375°F).
2. In a small bowl, mix together the olive oil, lemon juice, garlic, salt, pepper, rosemary, thyme, and oregano.
3. Clean the chicken by removing any excess fat and pat it dry with paper towels. Place the chicken in a roasting pan.
4. Rub the herb mixture all over the chicken, both outside and under the skin. Make sure the entire chicken is coated with the mixture.
5. Stuff the chicken cavity with the sliced lemons.
6. Roast the chicken in the preheated oven for about 60 minutes, or until the internal temperature reaches 75°C (165°F).
7. Remove the chicken from the oven and let it rest for about 10 minutes before carving.
8. Sprinkle the carved chicken with fresh parsley and serve.

Nutritional Information: Approximately 350 calories per serving, 32 g protein, 4 g carbohydrates, 22 g fat, 1 g fiber, 95 mg cholesterol, 650 mg sodium, 370 mg potassium.

Grilled Chicken Caesar Salad

Yield: 4 servings | Prep time: 15 minutes | Cook time: 15 minutes

Ingredients:

- 4 boneless, skinless chicken breasts (about 500g total)
- 1 tablespoon olive oil
- 1/2 teaspoon salt
- 1/4 teaspoon black pepper
- 2 heads romaine lettuce (about 500g total), chopped

- 100g cherry tomatoes, halved
- 50g grated Parmesan cheese
- 4 tablespoons low-fat Caesar dressing
- 1 lemon, cut into wedges
- Optional: whole grain croutons (about 40g, be mindful of portion size)

Directions:

1. Preheat the grill to medium-high heat. Brush the chicken breasts with olive oil, then season with salt and pepper.
2. Grill the chicken for 6-7 minutes per side, or until cooked through and the internal temperature reaches 75°C (165°F). Remove the chicken from the grill and let it rest for a few minutes before slicing.
3. In a large bowl, toss the chopped romaine lettuce and cherry tomatoes. Divide the salad among four plates.
4. Top each salad with grilled chicken slices, grated Parmesan cheese, and a tablespoon of low-fat Caesar dressing.
5. Garnish with lemon wedges and, if desired, add whole grain croutons for some added crunch (be mindful of portion size for carbohydrates).
6. Serve immediately.

Nutritional Information: Approximately 280 calories per serving, 30 g protein, 12 g carbohydrates, 12 g fat, 4 g fiber, 80 mg cholesterol, 700 mg sodium, 450 mg potassium.

Beef and Mushroom Stroganoff
Yield: 4 servings | Prep time: 15 minutes | Cook time: 20 minutes

Ingredients:

- 400g lean beef sirloin, sliced into thin strips
- Salt and pepper, to taste
- 1 tablespoon olive oil
- 1 medium onion (about 150g), chopped
- 3 cloves garlic, minced
- 300g mushrooms, sliced
- 2 tablespoons Worcestershire sauce
- 1 tablespoon Dijon mustard
- 240ml low-sodium beef broth
- 120g low-fat sour cream
- 2 tablespoons fresh parsley, chopped
- 200g whole wheat egg noodles, cooked according to package instructions

Directions:

1. Season the beef strips with salt and pepper.
2. In a large skillet, heat the olive oil over medium-high heat. Add the beef strips and brown them on all sides, about 3-4 minutes. Remove the beef from the skillet and set aside.
3. In the same skillet, add the chopped onion, garlic, and mushrooms. Sauté for about 5 minutes until the onions are translucent and the mushrooms are soft.
4. Stir in the Worcestershire sauce and Dijon mustard. Add the beef broth and bring the mixture to a simmer.
5. Return the beef strips to the skillet and simmer for an additional 2-3 minutes until the beef is cooked through.
6. Remove the skillet from the heat and stir in the sour cream and chopped parsley. Serve the stroganoff over the cooked whole wheat egg noodles.

Nutritional Information: Approximately 375 calories per serving, 30 g protein, 40 g carbohydrates, 12 g fat, 5 g fiber, 75 mg cholesterol, 350 mg sodium, 650 mg potassium.

Grilled Lamb Chops with Mint Chimichurri
Yield: 4 servings | Prep time: 15 minutes | Cook time: 10 minutes

Ingredients:

- 8 lamb chops (about 600g)
- Salt and pepper, to taste
- 2 tablespoons olive oil
- 1 bunch fresh mint (about 30g), chopped
- 1 bunch fresh parsley (about 30g), chopped
- 3 cloves garlic, minced
- 1 small red chilli, finely chopped
- 2 tablespoons red wine vinegar
- 60ml olive oil
- 1 tablespoon lemon juice
- Salt and pepper, to taste

Directions:

1. Preheat the grill to medium-high heat.
2. Season the lamb chops with salt and pepper, then drizzle with 2 tablespoons of olive oil. Place the lamb chops on the hot grill and cook for about 4-5 minutes on each side for medium-rare, or until they reach your desired level of doneness.
3. While the lamb chops are grilling, make the mint chimichurri. In a bowl, combine the chopped mint, parsley, minced garlic, chopped chilli, red wine vinegar, 60ml of olive oil, and lemon juice. Season with salt and pepper to taste, and mix well.
4. Once the lamb chops are done grilling, remove them from the grill and let them rest for a few minutes.
5. Serve the grilled lamb chops with a generous spoonful of the mint chimichurri.

Nutritional Information: Approximately 350 calories per serving, 24g protein, 3g carbohydrates, 27g fat, 1g fiber, 70mg cholesterol, 150mg sodium, 400mg potassium.

Chicken Piccata with Lemon Caper Sauce

Yield: 4 servings | Prep time: 15 minutes | Cook time: 25 minutes

Ingredients:

- 4 boneless, skinless chicken breasts (about 500g)
- Salt and pepper, to taste
- 2 tablespoons olive oil
- 2 cloves garlic, minced
- 250ml low-sodium chicken broth
- 60ml fresh lemon juice
- 2 tablespoons capers, rinsed and drained
- 2 tablespoons chopped fresh parsley
- 1 tablespoon unsalted butter
- Lemon slices, for garnish

Directions:

1. Season the chicken breasts with salt and pepper on both sides. Heat the olive oil in a large skillet over medium-high heat. Add the chicken breasts and cook for about 5-6 minutes on each side, until they are browned and cooked through. Remove the chicken from the skillet and set aside.
2. In the same skillet, add the minced garlic and cook for about 30 seconds, until fragrant. Add the chicken broth, lemon juice, and capers to the skillet. Bring the mixture to a simmer and cook for about 5 minutes, until the sauce has reduced slightly.
3. Return the chicken breasts to the skillet and cook for an additional 2-3 minutes, until they are heated through and coated with the sauce.
4. Remove the skillet from the heat and stir in the chopped parsley and unsalted butter. Serve the chicken breasts with the lemon caper sauce and garnish with lemon slices.

Nutritional Information: Approximately 250 calories per serving, 30g protein, 4g carbohydrates, 12g fat, 0g fiber, 80mg cholesterol, 400mg sodium, 300mg potassium.

Herb-Crusted Baked Trout

Yield: 4 servings | Prep time: 10 minutes | Cook time: 15 minutes

Ingredients:

- 4 trout fillets (about 150g each)
- 2 tablespoons olive oil
- 2 cloves garlic, minced
- 1 teaspoon fresh thyme, chopped
- 1 teaspoon fresh rosemary, chopped
- 1 teaspoon fresh parsley, chopped
- Zest of 1 lemon
- Salt and pepper, to taste
- Lemon wedges for serving

Directions:

1. Preheat your oven to 200°C (180°C fan-assisted). Line a baking tray with parchment paper.
2. In a small bowl, mix together the olive oil, garlic, thyme, rosemary, parsley, lemon zest, salt, and pepper.
3. Pat the trout fillets dry with paper towels. Place them on the prepared baking tray, skin-side down. Brush the herb mixture over the top of the fillets, coating them evenly.
4. Bake in the preheated oven for 12-15 minutes, or until the trout is cooked through and flakes easily with a fork.
5. Serve immediately with lemon wedges on the side.

Nutritional Information: Approximately 215 calories per serving, 28g protein, 1g carbohydrates, 11g fat, 0g fiber, 80mg cholesterol, 105mg sodium, 350mg potassium.

Stuffed Pork Tenderloin with Spinach and Feta

Yield: 4 servings | Prep time: 15 minutes | Cook time: 30 minutes

Ingredients:

- 1 pork tenderloin (about 500g)
- 150g fresh spinach, chopped
- 100g feta cheese, crumbled
- 2 cloves garlic, minced
- 1 tablespoon olive oil
- 1 teaspoon dried oregano
- Salt and pepper, to taste
- 50g sun-dried tomatoes, chopped
- 2 tablespoons chopped fresh parsley
- Toothpicks or kitchen twine for securing the tenderloin

Directions:

1. Preheat your oven to 200°C (180°C fan-assisted). In a skillet, heat the olive oil over medium heat. Add the garlic and sauté until fragrant. Add the chopped spinach and cook until wilted. Remove from heat, let it cool, and then mix in the feta cheese, sun-dried tomatoes, and oregano.
2. Butterfly the pork tenderloin by slicing it lengthwise down the center without cutting all the way through. Open it up and flatten it slightly with a meat mallet.
3. Season both sides of the tenderloin with salt and pepper. Spread the spinach and feta mixture evenly over one side of the tenderloin, leaving a small border around the edges. Roll up the tenderloin and secure it with toothpicks or kitchen twine.
4. Place the tenderloin in a baking dish and roast in the preheated oven for about 25-30 minutes, or until the internal temperature reaches 65°C.
5. Remove from the oven, cover with foil, and let it rest for about 5 minutes before slicing. Sprinkle with chopped parsley before serving.

Nutritional Information: Approximately 275 calories per serving, 35g protein, 5g carbohydrates, 13g fat, 2g fiber, 95mg cholesterol, 390mg sodium, 460mg potassium.

Moroccan Chicken with Couscous

Yield: 4 servings | Prep time: 15 minutes | Cook time: 40 minutes

Ingredients:

- 4 skinless, boneless chicken breasts (approx. 150 g each)
- 2 tablespoons olive oil
- 1 large onion, finely chopped
- 2 cloves garlic, minced
- 1 teaspoon ground cumin
- 1 teaspoon ground coriander
- 1 teaspoon ground paprika
- 1/2 teaspoon ground turmeric
- 1/2 teaspoon ground cinnamon
- 400 g canned chopped tomatoes
- 400 ml low-sodium chicken stock
- 150 g whole wheat couscous
- Salt and freshly ground black pepper, to taste
- 2 tablespoons fresh coriander, chopped
- 2 tablespoons fresh parsley, chopped
- 1 lemon, sliced for garnish

Directions:

1. In a large, deep skillet or Dutch oven, heat the olive oil over medium heat. Add the chicken breasts and cook for about 5 minutes on each side, or until they are browned. Remove the chicken breasts from the skillet and set them aside.
2. In the same skillet, add the chopped onion and cook for about 3 minutes, or until softened. Add the minced garlic, ground cumin, ground coriander, ground paprika, ground turmeric, and ground cinnamon. Cook for an additional 2 minutes, stirring constantly.
3. Add the chopped tomatoes and chicken stock to the skillet, stirring to combine. Bring the mixture to a simmer.
4. Return the chicken breasts to the skillet, nestling them into the sauce. Cover the skillet and reduce the heat to low. Cook for about 25 minutes, or until the chicken is cooked through.
5. While the chicken is cooking, prepare the couscous according to the package instructions. Fluff the couscous with a fork and season with salt and black pepper.
6. Serve the chicken breasts on a bed of couscous, topped with the tomato sauce. Garnish with chopped fresh coriander, parsley, and lemon slices.

Nutritional Information: Approximately 380 calories per serving, 35 g protein, 35 g carbohydrates, 9 g fat, 5 g fiber, 80 mg cholesterol, 250 mg sodium, 550 mg potassium.

Beef and Vegetable Stir Fry

Yield: 4 servings | Prep time: 15 minutes | Cook time: 20 minutes

Ingredients:

- 400 g lean beef steak, thinly sliced
- 1 tablespoon olive oil
- 1 medium onion, sliced
- 2 cloves garlic, minced
- 1 medium red bell pepper, sliced
- 1 medium yellow bell pepper, sliced
- 1 medium carrot, julienned
- 200 g broccoli florets
- 200 g sugar snap peas

- 2 tablespoons low-sodium soy sauce
- 1 tablespoon hoisin sauce
- 1 tablespoon oyster sauce
- 1 tablespoon water
- 1 teaspoon cornstarch
- Salt and freshly ground black pepper, to taste
- 2 tablespoons fresh coriander, chopped (optional)

Directions:

1. In a small bowl, whisk together the soy sauce, hoisin sauce, oyster sauce, water, and cornstarch. Set aside.
2. Heat the olive oil in a large nonstick skillet or wok over medium-high heat. Add the beef and cook for about 3-4 minutes, or until browned. Remove the beef from the skillet and set it aside.
3. In the same skillet, add the onion, garlic, red bell pepper, yellow bell pepper, and carrot. Cook for about 3 minutes, or until the vegetables begin to soften.
4. Add the broccoli and sugar snap peas to the skillet. Continue cooking for an additional 2-3 minutes, or until the vegetables are tender but still crisp.
5. Return the beef to the skillet. Pour the sauce over the beef and vegetables, stirring to coat. Cook for an additional 2 minutes, or until the sauce has thickened.
6. Season the stir fry with salt and black pepper, to taste. Serve the stir fry hot, garnished with chopped fresh coriander, if desired.

Nutritional Information: Approximately 250 calories per serving, 28 g protein, 15 g carbohydrates, 8 g fat, 3 g fiber, 70 mg cholesterol, 450 mg sodium, 600 mg potassium.

Balsamic Glazed Chicken with Roasted Vegetables
Yield: 4 servings | Prep time: 15 minutes | Cook time: 45 minutes

Ingredients:

For the chicken:
- 4 boneless, skinless chicken breasts (about 600 g)
- 1 tablespoon olive oil
- Salt and black pepper to taste
- 60 ml balsamic vinegar
- 1 tablespoon honey
- 1 teaspoon Dijon mustard
- 1 clove garlic, minced

For the roasted vegetables:
- 200 g carrots, peeled and cut into chunks
- 200 g Brussels sprouts, halved
- 200 g broccoli florets
- 2 tablespoons olive oil
- 1 teaspoon dried rosemary
- Salt and black pepper to taste

Directions:

1. Preheat the oven to 200°C (400°F).
2. In a small bowl, whisk together balsamic vinegar, honey, Dijon mustard, and minced garlic. Set aside.
3. In a large ovenproof skillet, heat 1 tablespoon of olive oil over medium heat. Season the chicken breasts with salt and pepper, then add them to the skillet. Cook the chicken for about 5 minutes on each side until browned. Remove from the heat.
4. Pour the balsamic glaze over the chicken breasts. Transfer the skillet to the oven and bake for about 15 minutes, or until the chicken is cooked through.
5. Meanwhile, in a large bowl, toss the carrots, Brussels sprouts, and broccoli with 2 tablespoons of olive oil, dried rosemary, salt, and black pepper. Spread the vegetables on a baking sheet in a single layer.
6. When the chicken has been in the oven for 15 minutes, add the baking sheet with the vegetables to the oven. Roast the vegetables for 25-30 minutes, stirring once or twice, until they are tender and browned.
7. Serve the chicken breasts with the roasted vegetables on the side.

Nutritional Information: Approximately 350 calories per serving, 35 g protein, 20 g carbohydrates, 14 g fat, 5 g fiber, 85 mg cholesterol, 370 mg sodium, 580 mg potassium.

Spicy Shrimp Tacos with Avocado Crema
Yield: 4 servings | Prep time: 15 minutes | Cook time: 10 minutes

Ingredients:

For the shrimp:
- 400g large shrimp, peeled and deveined
- 1 tablespoon olive oil
- 1 teaspoon chili powder
- 1/2 teaspoon smoked paprika
- 1/4 teaspoon cayenne pepper
- Salt and black pepper, to taste

For the avocado crema:
- 2 ripe avocados, pitted and peeled
- 125g Greek yogurt

- 1 clove garlic, minced
- Juice of 1 lime
- Salt and black pepper, to taste
- For the tacos:
- 8 small whole-grain tortillas (about 15cm diameter)
- 2 cups shredded lettuce
- 1 large tomato, diced
- 1/2 red onion, thinly sliced
- Fresh coriander, for garnish

Directions:

1. In a medium bowl, combine the shrimp with olive oil, chili powder, smoked paprika, cayenne pepper, salt, and black pepper. Toss until shrimp are evenly coated with the spices.
2. Heat a large skillet over medium-high heat. Cook the shrimp for 2-3 minutes on each side until they are opaque and cooked through. Remove from heat and set aside.
3. In a blender or food processor, combine the avocados, Greek yogurt, garlic, lime juice, salt, and black pepper. Blend until smooth and creamy.
4. To assemble the tacos, spread a generous amount of avocado crema on each tortilla. Top with shredded lettuce, diced tomato, and red onion. Place the cooked shrimp on top and garnish with fresh coriander.
5. Serve immediately and enjoy!

Nutritional Information: Approximately 350 calories per serving, 26 g protein, 33 g carbohydrates, 14 g fat, 9 g fiber, 125 mg cholesterol, 550 mg sodium, 850 mg potassium.

Delightful Desserts

Almond Flour Chocolate Brownies
Yield: 12 servings | Prep time: 15 minutes | Cook time: 25 minutes

Ingredients:

- 225g almond flour
- 50g unsweetened cocoa powder
- 100g erythritol or stevia (or other sugar substitute suitable for diabetics)
- 1 teaspoon baking powder
- 1/4 teaspoon salt
- 3 large eggs
- 100g unsalted butter, melted
- 1 teaspoon vanilla extract
- 100g unsweetened chocolate, chopped
- 60g chopped walnuts (optional)

Directions:

1. Preheat your oven to 180°C (160°C fan-assisted). Line a 20cm x 20cm baking tin with parchment paper.
2. In a large bowl, whisk together the almond flour, cocoa powder, erythritol or stevia, baking powder, and salt.
3. In a separate bowl, beat the eggs, melted butter, and vanilla extract until smooth. Add the wet ingredients to the dry ingredients and mix until well combined.
4. Fold in the chopped chocolate and walnuts, if using.
5. Spread the batter evenly into the prepared baking tin. Bake for 20-25 minutes, or until a toothpick inserted into the centre comes out with a few moist crumbs.
6. Allow the brownies to cool in the tin for about 10 minutes, then transfer to a wire rack to cool completely. Once cool, cut into 12 squares.

Nutritional Information: Approximately 230 calories per serving, 6g protein, 8g carbohydrates, 20g fat, 4g fiber, 60mg cholesterol, 80mg sodium, 150mg potassium.

No-Bake Strawberry and Cream Tart
Yield: 8 servings | Prep time: 25 minutes | Cook time: 0 minutes

Ingredients:

- 200g almond flour
- 100g unsweetened shredded coconut
- 80g melted coconut oil
- 4 tablespoons erythritol or stevia (or other sugar substitute suitable for diabetics)
- 250g strawberries, hulled and sliced
- 400g full-fat Greek yogurt
- Zest and juice of 1 lemon
- 1 teaspoon vanilla extract
- A pinch of salt

Directions:

1. In a medium mixing bowl, combine the almond flour, shredded coconut, melted coconut oil, and 2 tablespoons of erythritol or stevia. Mix until the mixture resembles wet sand. Press the mixture into the bottom and up the sides of a 23cm tart pan.
2. Place the tart pan in the fridge for 15 minutes to firm up.
3. In a separate mixing bowl, combine the Greek yogurt, remaining 2 tablespoons of erythritol or stevia, lemon zest, lemon juice, vanilla extract, and a pinch of salt. Mix until well combined.
4. Remove the tart pan from the fridge and spread the Greek yogurt mixture over the crust.
5. Top with sliced strawberries and refrigerate for at least 2 hours before serving.

Nutritional Information: Approximately 260 calories per serving, 8g protein, 10g carbohydrates, 22g fat, 4g fiber, 5mg cholesterol, 70mg sodium, 150mg potassium.

Lemon Ricotta Cheesecake
Yield: 8 servings | Prep time: 15 minutes | Cook time: 40 minutes

Ingredients:

- 500g ricotta cheese
- 150g erythritol or stevia (or other sugar substitute suitable for diabetics)
- 4 large eggs
- Zest and juice of 2 lemons
- 1 teaspoon vanilla extract
- 50g almond flour
- A pinch of salt

Directions:

1. Preheat your oven to 160°C (140°C fan-assisted). Grease a 23cm springform cake tin and line the bottom with parchment paper.
2. In a large mixing bowl, combine the ricotta cheese, erythritol or stevia, and eggs. Mix until smooth.
3. Add the lemon zest, lemon juice, vanilla extract, almond flour, and a pinch of salt. Mix until well combined.
4. Pour the mixture into the prepared cake tin and smooth the top with a spatula.
5. Bake in the preheated oven for 35-40 minutes, or until the edges are set but the center is still slightly jiggly.
6. Turn off the oven, open the door slightly, and let the cheesecake cool inside the oven for 1 hour.
7. Remove from the oven and let it cool to room temperature. Refrigerate for at least 4 hours or overnight before serving.

Nutritional Information: Approximately 180 calories per serving, 11g protein, 4g carbohydrates, 13g fat, 1g fiber, 120mg cholesterol, 130mg sodium, 170mg potassium.

Dark Chocolate Avocado Mousse
Yield: 4 servings | Prep time: 10 minutes | Cook time: 0 minutes

Ingredients:

- 2 ripe avocados, pitted and peeled
- 50g dark chocolate (minimum 70% cocoa), melted
- 3 tablespoons unsweetened cocoa powder
- 3 tablespoons erythritol or stevia (or other sugar substitute suitable for diabetics)
- 1 teaspoon vanilla extract
- A pinch of salt
- 100ml unsweetened almond milk

Directions:

1. Place the avocados in a food processor and blend until smooth.
2. Add the melted dark chocolate, cocoa powder, erythritol or stevia, vanilla extract, and a pinch of salt to the food processor. Blend until well combined.
3. Gradually add the almond milk, blending until the mixture reaches your desired consistency.
4. Spoon the mousse into serving glasses or bowls and refrigerate for at least 2 hours before serving.
5. Serve chilled, garnished with berries or a sprinkle of cocoa powder, if desired.

Nutritional Information: Approximately 230 calories per serving, 4g protein, 12g carbohydrates, 20g fat, 7g fiber, 0mg cholesterol, 40mg sodium, 550mg potassium.

Blueberry and Almond Crumble
Yield: 4 servings | Prep time: 10 minutes | Cook time: 30 minutes

Ingredients:

For the filling:
- 300g fresh blueberries
- 2 tablespoons erythritol or stevia (or other sugar substitute suitable for diabetics)
- 1 tablespoon lemon juice
- 1/2 teaspoon vanilla extract
- 1 tablespoon almond flour

For the crumble topping:
- 100g almond flour
- 30g rolled oats
- 30g unsalted butter, cold and cubed
- 2 tablespoons erythritol or stevia (or other sugar substitute suitable for diabetics)
- 1/4 teaspoon cinnamon

Directions:

1. Preheat your oven to 180°C (350°F).
2. In a medium bowl, combine the blueberries, erythritol or stevia, lemon juice, vanilla extract, and 1 tablespoon of almond flour. Transfer the mixture to a baking dish.
3. In another bowl, combine the almond flour, rolled oats, butter, erythritol or stevia, and cinnamon. Use your fingers to mix the ingredients until a crumbly texture is formed.
4. Sprinkle the crumble topping evenly over the blueberry mixture in the baking dish.
5. Bake for 25-30 minutes, or until the topping is golden brown and the blueberry filling is bubbling.
6. Allow the crumble to cool for a few minutes before serving. Enjoy with a dollop of Greek yogurt or a scoop of sugar-free ice cream, if desired.

Nutritional Information: Approximately 270 calories per serving, 8g protein, 18g carbohydrates, 20g fat, 5g fiber, 23mg cholesterol, 25mg sodium, 150mg potassium.

Sugar-free Chocolate Truffles
Yield: 12 truffles | Prep time: 10 minutes | Cook time: 5 minutes (plus 2 hours for chilling)

Ingredients:

- 150g unsweetened dark chocolate, finely chopped
- 80ml double cream
- 2 tablespoons erythritol or stevia (or other sugar substitute suitable for diabetics)
- 1/2 teaspoon vanilla extract
- Pinch of salt
- 1 tablespoon unsweetened cocoa powder, for dusting

Directions:

1. In a small saucepan, heat the double cream over medium heat until it just begins to simmer. Remove from heat.
2. Add the erythritol or stevia to the hot cream and stir until dissolved.
3. Place the chopped dark chocolate in a medium bowl and pour the hot cream mixture over it. Let it sit for a minute, then stir until smooth and glossy.
4. Add the vanilla extract and a pinch of salt, and stir to combine.
5. Cover the bowl with plastic wrap and place it in the refrigerator for at least 2 hours, or until the mixture is firm.
6. Once the mixture is firm, use a spoon or melon baller to scoop out small portions. Roll each portion into a ball using your hands, then roll each ball in the unsweetened cocoa powder to coat.
7. Store the truffles in an airtight container in the refrigerator until ready to serve. Enjoy!

Nutritional Information: Approximately 80 calories per truffle, 1g protein, 4g carbohydrates, 7g fat, 2g fiber, 8mg cholesterol, 2mg sodium, 100mg potassium.

Chia Seed and Berry Pudding

Yield: 4 servings | Prep time: 10 minutes | Cook time: 0 minutes (plus 4 hours for chilling)

Ingredients:

- 60g chia seeds
- 240ml unsweetened almond milk
- 1 tablespoon erythritol or stevia (or other sugar substitute suitable for diabetics)
- 1/2 teaspoon vanilla extract
- 150g mixed berries (such as strawberries, raspberries, blueberries)
- 15g unsweetened shredded coconut (optional)

Directions:

1. In a medium bowl, combine the chia seeds, unsweetened almond milk, erythritol or stevia, and vanilla extract. Stir until well mixed.
2. Cover the bowl with plastic wrap or a lid, and refrigerate for at least 4 hours, or overnight, until the mixture thickens and becomes a pudding-like consistency.
3. Before serving, give the pudding a good stir to ensure the chia seeds are evenly distributed.
4. Divide the pudding among 4 serving bowls or glasses, and top with the mixed berries and shredded coconut, if using.
5. Serve chilled and enjoy!

Nutritional Information: Approximately 120 calories per serving, 4g protein, 12g carbohydrates, 7g fat, 8g fiber, 0mg cholesterol, 60mg sodium, 100mg potassium.

Baked Apples with Cinnamon and Walnuts

Yield: 4 servings | Prep time: 10 minutes | Cook time: 40 minutes

Ingredients:

- 4 large apples, preferably tart varieties such as Granny Smith
- 80g chopped walnuts
- 1 tablespoon erythritol or stevia (or other sugar substitute suitable for diabetics)
- 1/2 teaspoon ground cinnamon
- 1/4 teaspoon ground nutmeg
- 120ml water

Directions:

1. Preheat the oven to 180°C (350°F).
2. Core the apples, leaving a small hole at the bottom to hold the filling. Place the apples in a baking dish.
3. In a small bowl, combine the chopped walnuts, erythritol or stevia, cinnamon, and nutmeg. Mix well.
4. Fill the cored apples with the walnut mixture, pressing the filling down slightly.
5. Pour the water into the bottom of the baking dish.
6. Bake the apples for 40 minutes, or until they are tender and the filling is golden brown.
7. Serve the baked apples warm, with the liquid from the baking dish spooned over them.

Nutritional Information: Approximately 160 calories per serving, 3g protein, 24g carbohydrates, 8g fat, 5g fiber, 0mg cholesterol, 2mg sodium, 200mg potassium.

Greek Yogurt Panna Cotta with Mixed Berries

Yield: 4 servings | Prep time: 10 minutes | Cook time: 10 minutes + 3 hours chilling time

Ingredients:

- 500g Greek yogurt
- 240ml milk
- 1 sachet (12g) gelatin powder
- 60ml water
- 3 tablespoons erythritol or stevia (or other sugar substitute suitable for diabetics)
- 1 teaspoon vanilla extract
- 300g mixed berries (blueberries, strawberries, raspberries)
- 1 tablespoon lemon juice
- Mint leaves for garnish (optional)

Directions:

1. In a small saucepan, combine the water and gelatin powder. Let it sit for 5 minutes to allow the gelatin to bloom.
2. Heat the saucepan over low heat, stirring until the gelatin is completely dissolved. Remove from heat.
3. In a large bowl, combine the Greek yogurt, milk, erythritol or stevia, and vanilla extract. Mix well.
4. Gradually whisk the dissolved gelatin into the yogurt mixture until smooth.
5. Divide the mixture among 4 dessert glasses or ramekins. Refrigerate for at least 3 hours or until set.
6. In a bowl, mix the mixed berries with the lemon juice.
7. When ready to serve, top the panna cotta with the mixed berries and garnish with mint leaves if desired.

Nutritional Information: Approximately 170 calories per serving, 14g protein, 15g carbohydrates, 6g fat, 2g fiber, 15mg cholesterol, 80mg sodium, 250mg potassium.

Almond and Coconut Macaroons

Yield: 12 servings | Prep time: 15 minutes | Cook time: 15 minutes

Ingredients:

- 200g unsweetened shredded coconut
- 100g almond flour
- 60g erythritol or stevia (or other sugar substitute suitable for diabetics)
- 2 large egg whites
- 1 teaspoon vanilla extract
- A pinch of salt

Directions:

1. Preheat your oven to 175°C (350°F). Line a baking sheet with parchment paper.
2. In a medium-sized mixing bowl, combine the shredded coconut, almond flour, and erythritol or stevia.
3. In a separate bowl, beat the egg whites with a pinch of salt until stiff peaks form.
4. Gently fold the egg whites and vanilla extract into the coconut and almond mixture until well combined.
5. Using a spoon, scoop out the mixture and form into small, rounded heaps on the prepared baking sheet.
6. Bake in the preheated oven for about 12-15 minutes or until the edges of the macaroons are golden brown.
7. Allow the macaroons to cool completely on the baking sheet before serving.

Nutritional Information: Approximately 110 calories per serving, 3g protein, 4g carbohydrates, 9g fat, 2g fiber, 0mg cholesterol, 20mg sodium, 60mg potassium.

No-Bake Peanut Butter and Chocolate Bars

Yield: 16 servings | Prep time: 15 minutes | Cook time: 0 minutes (Refrigerate for 2 hours)

Ingredients:

- 200g natural peanut butter (no added sugar or salt)
- 100g almond flour
- 50g erythritol or stevia (or other sugar substitute suitable for diabetics)
- 1 teaspoon vanilla extract
- A pinch of salt
- 150g sugar-free dark chocolate, chopped
- 2 tablespoons coconut oil

Directions:

1. In a medium-sized mixing bowl, combine the peanut butter, almond flour, erythritol or stevia, vanilla extract, and a pinch of salt. Mix until well combined.
2. Line a 20cm x 20cm (8x8-inch) baking dish with parchment paper, allowing some excess to hang over the edges for easy removal.
3. Press the peanut butter mixture into the bottom of the lined baking dish in an even layer.
4. In a microwave-safe bowl, combine the chopped sugar-free dark chocolate and coconut oil. Microwave in 20-second intervals, stirring after each interval, until the chocolate is melted and smooth.
5. Pour the melted chocolate over the peanut butter layer and spread it out evenly with a spatula.
6. Refrigerate the dish for at least 2 hours or until the chocolate has set.
7. Once set, lift the parchment paper to remove the bars from the dish. Cut into 16 squares and serve.

Nutritional Information: Approximately 180 calories per serving, 5g protein, 6g carbohydrates, 16g fat, 2g fiber, 0mg cholesterol, 55mg sodium, 130mg potassium.

Raspberry and Lemon Sorbet

Yield: 6 servings | Prep time: 15 minutes | Cook time: 0 minutes (Freeze for 4 hours)

Ingredients:

- 500g fresh raspberries
- 2 lemons, zested and juiced
- 100ml water
- 80g erythritol or stevia (or another suitable sugar substitute for diabetics)

Directions:

1. In a blender or food processor, blend the raspberries until smooth. If you prefer a smoother texture, you can strain the raspberry puree through a fine sieve to remove seeds, but this is optional.
2. In a separate bowl, combine the water and erythritol or stevia, stirring until dissolved. Add the lemon zest and juice and mix well.
3. Combine the raspberry puree with the lemon mixture and stir until well combined.
4. Pour the mixture into a freezer-safe container and freeze for at least 4 hours, stirring every hour to prevent large ice crystals from forming.
5. Once set, scoop out using an ice cream scoop and serve immediately.

Nutritional Information: Approximately 40 calories per serving, 1g protein, 10g carbohydrates, 0g fat, 4g fiber, 0mg cholesterol, 2mg sodium, 120mg potassium.

Vanilla and Berry Parfait
Yield: 4 servings | Prep time: 10 minutes | Cook time: 0 minutes

Ingredients:

- 300g Greek yogurt, low fat
- 1 tsp vanilla extract
- 1 tbsp stevia or erythritol (or other suitable sweetener for diabetics)
- 200g mixed berries (strawberries, blueberries, raspberries, blackberries)
- 40g almonds, chopped
- 2 tbsp chia seeds

Directions:

1. In a medium-sized bowl, mix Greek yogurt, vanilla extract, and sweetener until well combined.
2. In four serving glasses or bowls, layer the Greek yogurt mixture, berries, chopped almonds, and chia seeds in alternating layers. Start with the yogurt mixture at the bottom, then add a layer of berries, followed by almonds and chia seeds, and repeat.
3. Finish with a layer of berries and a sprinkle of chopped almonds on top.
4. Chill in the refrigerator for at least 1 hour before serving.

Nutritional Information: Approximately 130 calories per serving, 8g protein, 12g carbohydrates, 6g fat, 4g fiber, 4mg cholesterol, 25mg sodium, 180mg potassium.

Dark Chocolate and Raspberry Muffins
Yield: 12 servings | Prep time: 15 minutes | Cook time: 20 minutes

Ingredients:

- 200g whole wheat flour
- 40g unsweetened cocoa powder
- 1 tsp baking powder
- 1/2 tsp baking soda
- 1/4 tsp salt
- 2 large eggs
- 150g plain Greek yogurt
- 80ml unsweetened almond milk
- 80ml olive oil
- 100g xylitol (or sugar substitute)
- 1 tsp vanilla extract
- 100g fresh raspberries
- 50g dark chocolate chips

Directions:

1. Preheat the oven to 180°C (350°F) and line a muffin tin with paper liners.
2. In a large bowl, whisk together the whole wheat flour, cocoa powder, baking powder, baking soda, and salt.
3. In another bowl, beat the eggs and then mix in the Greek yogurt, almond milk, olive oil, xylitol, and vanilla extract until well combined.
4. Add the wet ingredients to the dry ingredients and gently mix until just combined. Do not overmix.
5. Gently fold in the fresh raspberries and dark chocolate chips.
6. Divide the batter evenly among the muffin cups, filling each about 2/3 full.
7. Bake in the preheated oven for 18-20 minutes, or until a toothpick inserted into the center of a muffin comes out clean.
8. Remove the muffins from the oven and allow them to cool in the tin for a few minutes before transferring them to a wire rack to cool completely.

Nutritional Information: Approximately 170 calories per serving, 5g protein, 18g carbohydrates, 10g fat, 3g fiber, 35mg cholesterol, 150mg sodium, 150mg potassium.

Baked Pear with Honey and Pecans
Yield: 4 servings | Prep time: 10 minutes | Cook time: 25 minutes

Ingredients:

- 4 ripe pears, halved and cored
- 4 tsp honey
- 40g pecans, chopped
- 1/2 tsp ground cinnamon
- 200g Greek yogurt, low fat, for serving

Directions:

1. Preheat your oven to 180°C (350°F).
2. Place the halved and cored pears in a baking dish, cut-side up. Drizzle each half with 1/2 tsp of honey and sprinkle with ground cinnamon.
3. Scatter the chopped pecans over the pears.
4. Bake for 25 minutes or until the pears are tender.
5. Serve the baked pears warm with a dollop of Greek yogurt on the side.

Nutritional Information: Approximately 170 calories per serving, 5g protein, 28g carbohydrates, 6g fat, 6g fiber, 0mg cholesterol, 10mg sodium, 220mg potassium.

Flourless Chocolate Cake
Yield: 6 servings | Prep time: 15 minutes | Cook time: 30 minutes

Ingredients:

- 200g dark chocolate (at least 70% cocoa), chopped
- 100g unsalted butter
- 4 large eggs, separated
- 75g granulated stevia or erythritol
- 1 tsp vanilla extract
- 1/4 tsp salt

Directions:

1. Preheat your oven to 180°C (350°F). Grease a 20cm (8-inch) round cake pan and line the bottom with parchment paper.
2. In a medium saucepan, melt the chocolate and butter over low heat, stirring until smooth. Remove from heat and let it cool slightly.
3. In a large bowl, beat the egg yolks with 50g of the sweetener and the vanilla extract until light and thick. Gradually stir in the melted chocolate mixture.
4. In another bowl, beat the egg whites with the salt until soft peaks form. Gradually add the remaining 25g of sweetener and continue beating until stiff peaks form.
5. Gently fold the egg whites into the chocolate mixture in three batches. Pour the batter into the prepared cake pan and spread it evenly.
6. Bake for 30 minutes or until the cake has risen and the top is firm to the touch. Allow the cake to cool completely in the pan on a wire rack before removing it.

Nutritional Information: Approximately 285 calories per serving, 7g protein, 12g carbohydrates, 24g fat, 3g fiber, 140mg cholesterol, 130mg sodium, 190mg potassium.

Lemon and Blueberry Frozen Yogurt

Yield: 6 servings | Prep time: 10 minutes | Cook time: 0 minutes (Freeze time: 4 hours)

Ingredients:

- 500g plain Greek yogurt
- 200g fresh or frozen blueberries
- 100ml lemon juice (about 2-3 lemons)
- Zest of 1 lemon
- 50g stevia or erythritol
- 1 tsp vanilla extract

Directions:

1. In a blender, combine the Greek yogurt, blueberries, lemon juice, lemon zest, sweetener, and vanilla extract. Blend until smooth.
2. Transfer the mixture into a freezer-safe container and spread it out evenly. Cover with a lid or plastic wrap and freeze for at least 4 hours or until firm.
3. Before serving, let the frozen yogurt sit at room temperature for a few minutes to soften slightly. Scoop into bowls and enjoy!

Nutritional Information: Approximately 95 calories per serving, 7g protein, 12g carbohydrates, 1g fat, 1g fiber, 5mg cholesterol, 35mg sodium, 130mg potassium.

Almond and Cherry Clafoutis

Yield: 6 servings | Prep time: 10 minutes | Cook time: 35 minutes

Ingredients:

- 400g fresh or frozen cherries, pitted
- 3 large eggs
- 250ml almond milk (unsweetened)
- 100g almond flour
- 50g stevia or erythritol
- 1 tsp vanilla extract
- 1/4 tsp almond extract
- Pinch of salt
- Almond flakes for garnish (optional)

Directions:

1. Preheat your oven to 180°C (350°F) and lightly grease a round baking dish with oil or butter.
2. In a large mixing bowl, whisk together the eggs, almond milk, almond flour, sweetener, vanilla extract, almond extract, and salt until well combined.
3. Arrange the cherries evenly at the bottom of the baking dish. Pour the batter over the cherries.
4. Bake for 35-40 minutes or until the clafoutis is set in the center and slightly golden on top.
5. Allow to cool for a few minutes, then garnish with almond flakes if desired. Serve warm or at room temperature.

Nutritional Information: Approximately 160 calories per serving, 8g protein, 12g carbohydrates, 10g fat, 3g fiber, 95mg cholesterol, 80mg sodium, 260mg potassium.

Cinnamon and Nutmeg Poached Pears

Yield: 4 servings | Prep time: 10 minutes | Cook time: 25 minutes

Ingredients:

- 4 ripe pears, peeled, halved, and cored
- 500ml water
- 2 cinnamon sticks
- 1/4 tsp ground nutmeg
- 1 tsp vanilla extract
- 1 tbsp stevia or erythritol
- A pinch of salt
- Optional: Zest of 1 lemon

Directions:

1. In a large saucepan, combine the water, cinnamon sticks, ground nutmeg, vanilla extract, sweetener, and salt. Bring to a gentle simmer over medium heat.
2. Add the peeled and cored pear halves to the simmering liquid. Cover the pan and let the pears poach for about 20 minutes, or until they are tender but not mushy. Make sure to turn the pears occasionally for even poaching.
3. Using a slotted spoon, remove the pears from the liquid and let them cool for a few minutes.
4. If desired, reduce the poaching liquid until it thickens slightly to create a syrup. Discard the cinnamon sticks.
5. Serve the poached pears warm or chilled, drizzled with the reduced syrup, and garnished with lemon zest if desired.

Nutritional Information: Approximately 100 calories per serving, 1g protein, 27g carbohydrates, 0g fat, 6g fiber, 0mg cholesterol, 40mg sodium, 220mg potassium.

Printed in Great Britain
by Amazon

31598175R00053